AFRICA 101

The Pan African Lifestyle Guide to Relocating, Investing and Living the African Dream in the Motherland.

By Emmanuel Bope and Solange Bope

CANADA

PAN AFRICAN LIFESTYLE INC.

Authors: Emmanuel Bope and Solange Bope

Featured Expert: Kea Wakesho Simmons

Printed and bound in Canada

First printing Marh 2023

Published by PAN AFRICAN LIFESTYLE Inc.

Calgary, Alberta

ISBN   978-1-998780-13-6   Paperback

www.panafricanlifestyle.com

The African Dream is the pursuit, fulfillment, and enjoyment of the highest quality of life and lifestyle in the Motherland.

FOREWORD

It is with immense pride and joy that I write this foreword for *Africa 101: The Pan African Lifestyle Guide to Relocating, Investing & Living The African Dream in the Motherland*. This book is more than just a guide; it is a bold invitation to all of us who long to reconnect with our roots, discover new opportunities, and embrace the life we deserve in Africa.

As the founder of *Traverze Culture*, I've had the privilege of working closely with Emmanuel Bope and Solange Bope, visionaries, brilliant digital marketing strategists, and business minds who have consistently led with purpose, determination, and a deep love for the African continent. Their unwavering commitment to uplifting Pan-Africanism through their innovative work at *Pan African Lifestyle* (PAL) is a testament to their forward-thinking approach and their dedication to fostering connections across the African diaspora.

Through PAL, they have created a platform that not only celebrates the richness of African culture but also provides the tools and knowledge necessary for the global Black diaspora to thrive on the Motherland. The essence of *Africa 101* is deeply rooted in a philosophy and practice that I coined as *Afrocentric*

Regenerative Travel, a concept that embodies collaboration, community, and conscious capitalism. It is this philosophy that drives the mission behind *Traverze Culture*, and I am proud to see it reflected in the work of Emmanuel and Solange. Their approach to leading *Pan African Lifestyle* with innovation, collaboration, and sustainability is an inspiring example of how we can create and sustain businesses that not only thrive but also uplift communities and promote collective success.

PAL's mission, in partnership with *Traverze Culture*, is to open doors for people who want to make Africa their home, whether by relocating, investing, or simply immersing themselves in the continent's vibrant and diverse ways of life. It's about more than just visiting Africa; it's about cultivating a lifestyle that celebrates who we are as Africans and the tremendous opportunities that await us.

This book, *Africa 101*, is the natural next step in that journey. It stands as a comprehensive guide, meticulously crafted to support those who are ready to embrace The African Dream. From the practicalities of relocation to navigating investment opportunities, this guide covers it all. Emmanuel and Solange have curated a resource that will equip you with the knowledge and confidence to make informed decisions about your future in Africa.

The African Dream, as I see it, is the pursuit of the highest quality of life, an empowered, authentic existence that celebrates culture, entrepreneurship, and the shared success of the African diaspora. It's about finding your place in the Motherland, building businesses that contribute to the economy, and living a lifestyle that is fulfilling, abundant, and rooted in community. This book is your roadmap to living that dream.

The importance of this book cannot be overstated. In a world where the narrative surrounding Africa is often incomplete or misrepresented, *Africa 101* provides an authentic and insightful view of what it truly means to live, work, and thrive on the continent. It empowers us to make choices that align with our aspirations, whether that means acquiring property, building businesses, or enjoying the lifestyle and cultural richness that only Africa can offer. This is The African Dream.

As you turn these pages, I encourage you to take this opportunity to envision your future on the continent. Let this book be your source of inspiration and practical advice, guiding you as you embrace the possibilities that await. The Motherland is calling, and now is the time to answer.

Here's to your journey. Here's to your Pan-African lifestyle and your enjoyment of The African Dream.

With pride and gratitude,

Kea Wakesho Simmons

Kea Wakesho Simmons

Founder, *Traverze Culture*
Certified Medical Tourism Facilitator

DEDICATION

To all Pan African Lifestylers (PALs), the dreamers, the doers, and the visionaries who believe in the boundless potential of Africa. This book is for you, a guide to not just imagining The African Dream, but living it boldly and unapologetically.

To Alvin Harris, whose visionary idea sparked the creation of this book and the subsequent course. Your insight and belief in this mission have been invaluable, and we are grateful for your role in bringing this to life.

To Kea Wakesho Simmons, a powerhouse of wisdom, mentorship, and unwavering partnership. Your leadership in Traverze Culture and your philosophy of Afrocentric Regenerative Travel have deeply influenced our work, inspiring us to build something transformative for the global Black diaspora.

To our incredible Pan African Lifestyle team, your dedication, creativity, and commitment to the movement have been the driving force behind Pan African Lifestyle's success. We are beyond thankful for your contributions in making this vision a reality.

And to the extended team of travel advisors and industry professionals who have played a role in shaping this guide, your expertise and passion for Africa's travel, investment, and lifestyle industries have helped us create a resource that will empower countless individuals to call Africa home.

This book is more than just words on a page, it is a movement, a roadmap, and a testament to the power of collective vision. May it inspire generations to come.

CONTENTS

CHAPTER DETAILS

This guide is designed for members of the global Black diaspora who are eager to relocate, invest, and build a fulfilling life in Africa. Whether you seek citizenship, business opportunities, or cultural reconnection, this book provides practical steps, insights, and essential knowledge to thrive on the continent.

Chapter 1: Preparing Your Mindset for the Motherland
Before making the move to Africa, it is essential to shift your perspective and develop the right mindset. This chapter explores the mental and emotional preparation required to transition successfully.

Key Topics:
- **Overcoming Misconceptions** – Understanding the realities of African life beyond media stereotypes.
- **Embracing Cultural Differences** – Learning about traditional customs, values, and social etiquette.
- **The Pan-African Vision** – How returning or investing in Africa contributes to the continent's progress.

- **Adapting to New Challenges** – Preparing for lifestyle changes, infrastructure differences, and bureaucratic processes.
- **Building Resilience** – Developing patience, flexibility, and a problem-solving attitude for a smoother transition.

Chapter 2: Choosing Your Ideal African Destination

With 54 diverse countries, Africa offers a wide range of relocation options. This chapter helps you identify the best country based on your personal and professional goals.

Key Topics:
- **Factors to Consider** – Safety, cost of living, economic opportunities, climate, and lifestyle.
- **Country Spotlights** – A deep dive into popular relocation hubs like Ghana, Nigeria, Rwanda, South Africa, Kenya, and Tanzania.
- **Language & Communication** – Understanding the impact of language barriers and how to navigate them.
- **Urban vs. Rural Living** – The pros and cons of settling in major cities versus smaller towns or villages.

- **Visa & Residency Requirements** – A general overview of entry and long-term stay requirements across different countries.

Chapter 3: Citizenship & Residency Pathways
Understanding the legal processes of becoming a resident or citizen in Africa is crucial. This chapter provides an overview of different pathways to securing legal status.

Key Topics:
- **Dual Citizenship & Naturalization** – Countries that allow dual nationality and the requirements for becoming a citizen.
- **Repatriation Programs** – Special pathways for African descendants (e.g., Ghana's Year of Return & Right of Abode).
- **Investment & Business-Based Residency** – How investing in real estate or business can secure residency.
- **Long-Term Visa & Work Permits** – Options for digital nomads, retirees, and entrepreneurs.
- **Legal Requirements & Paperwork** – What documents you need and how to navigate government bureaucracy.

Chapter 4: Financial Planning & Building Wealth in Africa

Managing finances effectively is critical to thriving in Africa. This chapter covers budgeting, banking, investment strategies, and wealth-building opportunities.

Key Topics:

- **Cost of Living** – How to budget for housing, transportation, food, and healthcare.
- **Banking & Money Transfers** – Setting up local bank accounts, mobile money, and international transfers.
- **Investment Opportunities** – Key sectors to invest in (real estate, agriculture, tourism, tech, etc.).
- **Entrepreneurship in Africa** – How to start and grow a business on the continent.
- **Managing Risks** – Protecting your assets and understanding economic fluctuations.

Chapter 5: Finding Housing & Settling In

Securing a home is one of the most important steps in relocating. This chapter provides guidance on finding and securing accommodation.

Key Topics:
- **Renting vs. Buying Property** – Pros and cons of each option and how to avoid scams.
- **Understanding Local Real Estate Markets** – Housing trends in different African regions.
- **Negotiating Lease Agreements** – What to look for in rental contracts.
- **Building a Home** – The process of purchasing land and constructing a house.
- **Essential Services & Utilities** – How to set up water, electricity, internet, and security.

Chapter 6: Business & Employment Opportunities

Africa is full of economic opportunities, but understanding the job market and business environment is key. This chapter guides professionals, entrepreneurs, and investors.

Key Topics:
- **Job Market Overview** – High-demand industries and employment opportunities.
- **Starting a Business** – Legal requirements, business registration, and funding options.
- **Networking & Professional Growth** – How to connect with like-minded professionals and business communities.

- **Challenges & Solutions** – Common business hurdles and how to overcome them.
- **Side Hustles & Remote Work** – Digital opportunities and freelancing options.

Chapter 7: Healthcare, Safety & Wellness

Ensuring good health and safety is essential when moving to a new country. This chapter helps you navigate the African healthcare system and stay safe.

Key Topics:
- **Understanding the Healthcare System** – Private vs. public hospitals and quality of care.
- **Health Insurance & Medical Costs** – Options for expats and repatriates.
- **Vaccinations & Preventative Care** – Necessary shots and medications before and after arrival.
- **Safety & Security** – Tips for personal security, avoiding scams, and navigating law enforcement.
- **Mental & Emotional Well-Being** – How to manage homesickness, culture shock, and stress.

Chapter 8: Education & Raising a Family in Africa
For those relocating with children, this chapter provides insights into the African education system and family-friendly living.

Key Topics:
- **Types of Schools** – Public, private, and international school options.
- **Homeschooling & Alternative Education** – Exploring non-traditional education pathways.
- **Cost of Education** – School fees and budgeting for education.
- **Family & Community Life** – Raising children in an African cultural environment.
- **Dual Identity & Cultural Integration** – Helping children adapt to their new home.

Chapter 9: Travel, Exploration & Enjoying African Culture
One of the greatest joys of living in Africa is exploring its rich cultures, landscapes, and traditions. This chapter focuses on travel, entertainment, and lifestyle.

Key Topics:

- **Top Travel Destinations** – Must-visit cities, beaches, national parks, and cultural sites.
- **Transportation & Getting Around** – Options for local and international travel.
- **Social Life & Entertainment** – Music, nightlife, festivals, and cultural events.
- **Food & Culinary Experiences** – The best local cuisines and dining experiences.
- **Building Community** – How to integrate into local and expat communities.

Chapter 10: Sustaining The African Dream

Once settled, how can you continue thriving and embracing a fulfilling lifestyle in Africa? This final chapter focuses on long-term success, well-being, and fully enjoying life in the Motherland.

Key Topics:

- **Building Wealth & Creating Legacy** – Strategies for financial freedom, smart investments, and securing a prosperous future.

- **Embracing a Pan-African Lifestyle** – Immersing in Africa's diverse cultures, travel, and experiences for a rich and fulfilling life.

- **Wellness & Community** – Prioritizing health, meaningful relationships, and a balanced lifestyle in the Motherland.

Final Thoughts

Africa is not just a place to relocate; it's a place to build a meaningful life, contribute, and grow. This guide provides the foundation needed to embark on your journey with confidence and purpose.

DISCLAIMER

The information provided in *Africa 101: The Pan African Lifestyle Guide to Relocating, Investing & Living The African Dream in the Motherland* serves as essential foundational knowledge for those looking to travel, relocate, or invest in Africa. While we strive to offer accurate and insightful guidance, this book is not a substitute for professional advice.

We strongly recommend consulting with qualified professionals, including doctors, lawyers, and financial experts, before making any commitments related to travel, relocation, or investment. Every individual's circumstances are unique, and seeking expert opinions will help ensure well-informed and responsible decision-making as you embark on your journey to living The African Dream.

For those who need additional support, we have a team of professional experts ready to assist. Feel free to email **info@panafricanlifestyle.com** or visit **panafricanlifestyle.com** and fill out the contact form to get personalized guidance.

PREFACE

Fellow Pan African Lifestylers (PALs), let it be known that the vision and cause of The African Dream is one of liberty, self-governance, and the unwavering pursuit of prosperity. No person of African descent can truly be free unless they have dominion over their own affairs, control the fruits of their labor, and stand firm against the forces of division and oppression that have long sought to undermine our people worldwide. The only true solution to these injustices is for Africans, at home and across the diaspora, to actualize The African Dream in the Motherland.

The African Dream is one of unity, independence, and enterprise. It is not granted by foreign powers nor secured through the goodwill of others—it must be forged by our own strength, wisdom, and perseverance. True self-determination begins when we reclaim our birthright and build Africa on our own terms. Just as great nations have risen through enterprise and collective economic power, so too must Africa rise—not as a subject of foreign interests, but as the master of its own destiny, empowered by those who choose to live The African Dream in Africa.

To uplift our people, we must be intentional about creating a thriving and sustainable future. The cause of Africa is just, and when pursued with steadfastness and virtue, justice will always prevail. The foundation of Africa's success lies in a strong and prosperous middle class, a flourishing business elite, and a network of Pan-African professionals, entrepreneurs, retirees, and creatives committed to living and investing in The African Dream.

If Africa is to be great, let it be through industry and self-reliance. If Africa is to be free, let it be through unbreakable unity. If Africa is to endure, let it be through the unshakable spirit of its people—no longer subject to external rule, but standing as rightful stewards of their lands, their futures, and their legacies.

The African Dream is not a distant hope or an abstract concept—it is a responsibility, a movement, and a reality that is being built today. It is the vision of a self-sufficient, prosperous, and united Africa, where its people harness their vast potential to create thriving economies, strong institutions, and a future defined by dignity and opportunity. It is a dream of innovation, where African solutions drive global progress. A dream of cultural pride, where the continent's rich heritage is celebrated, and its narratives are shaped by its own people.

But this dream does not come easily. It requires action, resilience, and a commitment to dismantling barriers—both historical and self-imposed. It demands leadership rooted in service, economies built on equity, and the collective belief that Africa's greatest wealth is not its resources, but its people. The African Dream is about self-determination, breaking cycles of dependency, and reclaiming Africa's rightful place as a global leader in business, technology, culture, and governance. It is about a continent where young people have the tools and opportunities to succeed, where borders connect rather than divide, and where unity empowers rather than weakens.

The dream of living The African Dream is not just an aspiration—it is a call to action. For generations, the global Black diaspora has sought ways to reconnect with the Motherland, rediscover the places where our stories began, and build a future rooted in our shared heritage.

That is why *Africa 101: The Pan African Lifestyle Guide to Relocating, Investing & Living The African Dream in the Motherland* was created. This guide is designed to help you take the first step toward making this dream a reality. It is for those ready to embark on a transformative journey—to relocate, explore citizenship pathways, invest in Africa's booming economies, and immerse themselves in its diverse cultures. Inside, you will find essential insights, practical steps, and expert advice to navigate the complexities of moving to and thriving in Africa.

Whether you seek to build a business, establish a home, reconnect with your roots, or simply embrace the opportunities Africa offers, this guide equips you with the knowledge to make informed decisions. More than a resource on logistics, this book is a blueprint for those who wish to honor their ancestry, contribute to Africa's future, and live in alignment with the values of community, growth, and empowerment.

Africa is calling. This is your guide to answering. Let it be your roadmap to success in the Motherland, your key to unlocking Africa's potential, and your invitation to be part of the powerful, ever-growing legacy of The African Dream.

Welcome home, where opportunity meets destiny.

Emmanuel Bope and Solange Bope

Emmanuel Bope and Solange Bope

Founders, *Pan African Lifestyle*

INTRODUCTION

By Kea Wakesho Simmons

Welcome to *Africa 101: The Pan-African Lifestyle Guide to Relocating, Investing & Living the African Dream in the Motherland*—your ultimate roadmap to thriving on the African continent. Whether you are seeking to reconnect with your roots, explore new opportunities, or establish a long-term presence in Africa, this guide provides the essential knowledge and practical steps to make your transition smooth and successful.

Africa is a land of immense possibilities, offering rich cultures, economic growth, and a sense of belonging that many in the global Black diaspora have long yearned for. With 54 diverse countries, each with its own unique landscape, opportunities, and lifestyle, choosing the right path can be overwhelming. This guide simplifies that process, equipping you with the insights and tools needed to navigate your journey with confidence. Before navigating this journey, it is important to do so with the right mindset and intent.

Afrocentric Regenerative Travel

I am Kea Wakesho Simmons, founder of Traverze Culture, a seasoned travel and relocation expert, certified medical tourism facilitator, and former military corps member with a background in HR. My passion for travel was ignited during my deployments, where I witnessed the power of cultural exchange firsthand. This passion evolved into a mission: to connect the global Black diaspora with their roots, particularly in Kenya, through travel, relocation, and medical tourism.

Throughout my career, I have encountered various tourism models—sustainable tourism, regenerative tourism, and eco-tourism. While these frameworks promote responsible travel and environmental stewardship, they often lack a crucial element: an Afrocentric perspective that prioritizes the lived experiences, aspirations, and economic empowerment of both the African diaspora and those on the continent. That's why I developed Afrocentric Regenerative Travel (ART)—a groundbreaking approach that centers on community, collaboration, and conscious capitalism to foster meaningful, sustainable connections with the motherland.

What Is Afrocentric Regenerative Travel?

Afrocentric Regenerative Travel (ART) is more than just a travel philosophy—it is a movement that redefines how the global Black diaspora engages with Africa. Unlike traditional tourism, which often extracts value from host communities without reinvesting in them, ART focuses on reciprocal exchange and collective growth. It is about forging deep, lasting bonds between diasporans and local Africans in ways that uplift both sides culturally, socially, and economically.

ART is rooted in three core principles:

1. **Exchange:** Diasporans bring their skills, knowledge, and global experience, while those on the continent share their wisdom, culture, and local expertise.

2. **Integration:** Travel and relocation should be done with the intent to integrate into African societies, understanding the systems, customs, and opportunities that exist at personal, professional, local, and continental levels.

3. **Collaboration:** By partnering with African entrepreneurs, creatives, and communities, diasporans can co-create solutions that drive

economic independence and cultural enrichment.

ART and Conscious Capitalism

At its core, ART aligns with the principles of conscious capitalism. While capitalism in its conventional form has often exploited African nations and their resources, conscious capitalism offers a path to ethical, sustainable development. This approach ensures that businesses and individuals engage in economic activities that prioritize social impact, fair exchange, and community upliftment.

Through ART, we encourage diasporans not just to travel but to invest—whether in real estate, agribusiness, tech startups, or social enterprises. Rather than seeing Africa as a place for short-term visits, we promote long-term engagement where tourism leads to business opportunities, job creation, and infrastructure development.

The Pan-African Lifestyle and The African Dream

Living a Pan-African lifestyle and achieving The African Dream require intentionality. This means engaging in meaningful cultural exchanges where both parties—the diaspora and the continent—mutually benefit.

- **For the diaspora**, this means immersing themselves in local cultures, learning indigenous languages, understanding the political and economic landscapes, and forming genuine relationships.

- **For those on the continent**, this means welcoming diasporans not as foreigners but as long-lost relatives returning home. It means sharing knowledge about land ownership, business regulations, and local networks to ensure diasporans thrive and contribute positively.

By embracing ART, we dismantle the traditional tourist-consumer model and replace it with a co-creation model where every traveler is also a builder, an investor, and a collaborator.

Moving Forward with ART

The time has come to move beyond surface-level tourism and embrace Afrocentric Regenerative Travel as the blueprint for how we engage with Africa. ART is the bridge that reconnects the diaspora with their ancestral lands—not just for nostalgia but for the creation of a future where Africa and its people, at home and abroad, flourish together.

Africa 101

Join me in championing this movement, where travel is no longer a mere journey but a transformative experience rooted in growth, empowerment, and legacy-building. This is the future of travel. This is Afrocentric Regenerative Travel.

Who This Guide is For

This book is designed for members of the global Black diaspora who are eager to relocate, invest, or immerse themselves in Africa's vast opportunities. Whether you are:

- A professional or entrepreneur looking to expand your business in African markets,

- A digital nomad or retiree seeking a new way of life,

- A family desiring to raise children in an environment that reflects their heritage,

- A Pan-Africanist committed to building a stronger Black global economy,

- Or an individual simply looking to explore, travel, and experience the continent's beauty—

This guide is tailored to provide you with clear, actionable steps to make your dreams a reality.

What You'll Learn

Relocating to Africa is more than just a change of address; it is a transformative experience that requires the right mindset, preparation, and strategy. In this guide, you will discover:

- **How to mentally and emotionally prepare for life in Africa** – Overcoming misconceptions, embracing cultural differences, and building resilience.

- **How to choose the best country for your needs** – Exploring factors such as safety, cost of living, business opportunities, and lifestyle.

- **How to navigate citizenship and residency pathways** – Understanding visas, dual nationality, and repatriation programs.

- **How to build financial stability and wealth in Africa** – Managing finances, finding investment opportunities, and launching a business.

- **How to secure housing and settle into your new home** – Renting, buying property, and understanding local real estate markets.

- **How to access employment and entrepreneurial opportunities** – Navigating the job market, professional networking, and starting a business.

- **How to ensure health, safety, and overall well-being** – Understanding healthcare systems, security measures, and mental wellness.

- **How to raise and educate children in Africa** – Schooling options, cultural integration, and family life.

- **How to explore, travel, and fully embrace the African experience** – Discovering the continent's diverse landscapes, food, entertainment, and communities.

- **How to sustain the African dream long-term** – Building wealth, maintaining cultural immersion, and securing a prosperous future.

A Movement Towards a Global Black Future

Africa is not just a destination—it is a movement, a lifestyle, and an opportunity to contribute to a thriving future. The continent is evolving, with rapid economic growth, innovation, and a resurgence of African identity. By relocating, investing, or engaging with Africa, you are not only fulfilling personal goals but also playing a vital role in shaping the future of the Black world.

Through this guide, you will be equipped with the knowledge, strategies, and inspiration to make informed decisions about your journey to Africa. Whether you are taking your first step in researching or you are ready to book your flight, *Africa 101* is here to support you at every stage.

Let's embark on this journey together—toward a fulfilling, prosperous, and impactful life in the Motherland.

CHAPTER ONE

PREPARING YOUR MINDSET FOR THE MOTHERLAND

"The one who asks questions doesn't lose their way," an African proverb, highlights the vital role that curiosity and the pursuit of knowledge play in guiding one's journey. It emphasizes that by asking questions, individuals are better equipped to navigate challenges, make informed decisions, and stay on the right path. Seeking clarity and understanding through inquiry not only enriches one's perspective but also fosters growth, ensuring that the journey is purposeful and direction-oriented. In this way, questioning becomes an essential tool for success and personal development.

Before making the bold decision to move to Africa, it is essential to shift your perspective and mentally prepare yourself for the transition. This shift is about embracing not only a new place but also a new way of thinking. The following chapter explores the critical mental and emotional preparations necessary for a successful move to Africa, ensuring that you approach this life-changing experience with an open mind, resilience, and respect for the continent's vast diversity.

Overcoming Misconceptions

Africa is often portrayed in the media through a limited and distorted lens, focusing primarily on poverty, conflict, and disease. While these challenges are real, they do not define the continent as a whole. Africa is a land of incredible diversity, composed of 54 countries, each with its own history, culture, and identity. To overcome these misconceptions, it's essential to engage with multiple perspectives. Instead of relying on mainstream media, seek out literature, documentaries, and firsthand accounts that highlight Africa's rich cultural heritage, successes, and everyday life. One of the best ways to break free from stereotypes is to interact directly with locals. Building relationships with African communities will provide you with authentic insights that you won't find in the media. Additionally, traveling to various regions across the continent will expose you to Africa's true complexities, offering you a more comprehensive understanding of its various societies and cultures.

Embracing Cultural Differences

Africa's cultural diversity is one of its most exciting aspects, but it also requires a thoughtful approach. The continent is home to hundreds of languages, customs, and traditions, and it's important to respect these differences as you immerse yourself in local life. One practical way to begin embracing cultural differences is by learning local languages. While many Africans are multilingual, speaking a local language can significantly enhance your interactions and demonstrate your respect for the community. Social etiquette also varies widely, and understanding these nuances is key to forming positive relationships. For example, in Southern Africa, it's customary to receive items with both hands cupped together as a sign of respect, and in many places, it may be considered impolite to use your left hand for certain tasks. Participating in cultural practices, such as attending local festivals or observing traditional ceremonies, will also deepen your understanding and appreciation of the social values and customs that shape daily life.

The Pan-African Vision

At the heart of the African experience is Pan-Africanism, a movement that unites people of African descent across the globe, emphasizing solidarity, unity, and the shared goal of empowerment. Rooted in the history of colonialism, resistance, and the fight for independence, Pan-Africanism envisions a world where Africans, both on the continent and in the diaspora, work together for collective progress. As you prepare for your move, it is essential to understand and appreciate the significance of this movement. Recognizing the shared histories and experiences of Africans can inspire a sense of connection and purpose. Investing in or returning to Africa means contributing to its development, not as an outsider but as someone who is part of a larger movement for economic growth, cultural renaissance, and social justice. The Pan-African vision is not just about return or investment; it's about supporting the continent's long-term progress through collaboration and active participation.

Adapting to New Challenges

Transitioning to life in Africa can be both exhilarating and challenging. One of the most significant differences you may encounter is the varying levels of infrastructure across different countries and regions. While some urban areas boast modern amenities and efficient public transport, rural regions may face challenges such as inconsistent access to electricity, water, or healthcare. Being adaptable and having a flexible attitude will help you navigate these differences. The pace of life can also be a stark contrast to what you may be used to, with some areas embracing a slower, more communal rhythm. Bureaucratic processes may also be different from those in Western countries, and it's essential to be prepared for delays or complexities in legal and administrative matters. Understanding that things may not always go as planned is an important part of adapting to a new lifestyle. Embracing these challenges with an open heart will help you make the most of the experience, allowing you to grow both personally and professionally.

Building Resilience

Resilience is a key trait that will serve you well in the face of any challenges you encounter while adjusting to life in Africa. The ability to remain patient, flexible, and solution-oriented is crucial when adapting to a new environment. The systems and processes in Africa may not always operate according to the predictable patterns you're used to, but by maintaining a positive and adaptable mindset, you can navigate these challenges with ease. Resilience is also about being proactive and resourceful in finding solutions, whether that means learning new skills, seeking local guidance, or simply exercising patience. Additionally, it's helpful to build a support network of fellow expatriates, local communities, or organizations that can provide assistance when needed. This support system will be invaluable as you work through the inevitable ups and downs of living in a new country. By developing resilience, you'll not only survive the transition—you'll thrive in it.

In conclusion, preparing your mindset for life in Africa is about more than just intellectual understanding; it's about emotional readiness. Shifting your perspective and embracing the complexities of Africa will ensure that your transition is not only successful but also deeply enriching. With the right mindset, you can approach the continent with respect, openness, and a genuine desire to contribute to its progress, all while enjoying the unique opportunities that life in Africa has to offer.

CHAPTER TWO

CHOOSING YOUR IDEAL AFRICAN DESTINATION

*The African proverb **"Only a fool dips his two feet in water"** suggests that one should approach situations with caution and not rush into things without full understanding or preparation. It warns against jumping into unknown or risky ventures without careful consideration. The proverb emphasizes the importance of thinking through decisions and recognizing the potential consequences before taking action.*

With 54 diverse nations, Africa presents an array of relocation opportunities, each with its own economic strengths, cultural nuances, and lifestyle advantages. Choosing the right destination requires careful consideration of personal aspirations, professional opportunities, and practical realities. This chapter serves as a guide to help you make an informed decision about where to settle on the continent. While Africa is filled with incredible countries to explore, we have chosen to highlight a selection of popular destinations based on the interests of our audience and surveys we have conducted.

Relocating to Africa is an exciting prospect, but it demands a comprehensive understanding of the conditions that will shape your experience. Among the most critical considerations are safety and stability, as political climates and crime rates vary across the continent. Researching government policies, law enforcement efficiency, and healthcare accessibility will help ensure a secure transition. The cost of living is another crucial factor, with significant differences between countries and cities. Some locations offer a luxurious lifestyle at lower costs, while others mirror expenses found in major Western metropolises.

Economic and career opportunities also play a role, particularly for those seeking employment, starting a business, or investing. Understanding each country's economic climate, dominant industries, and business regulations is essential. Climate and geography should also be considered, as Africa's diverse climate zones range from arid deserts to tropical rainforests. Finally, factors such as healthcare infrastructure, educational institutions, technological development, and access to modern amenities contribute to the overall quality of life in different countries.

To simplify the decision-making process, we have spotlighted eight countries that are frequently cited as top destinations for expatriates, repatriates, and entrepreneurs seeking to relocate to Africa. **Kenya** is the economic engine of East Africa, attracting investors, digital entrepreneurs, and professionals. Nairobi, the capital, is home to a flourishing tech industry known as the "Silicon Savannah," while Mombasa offers a more relaxed, tropical lifestyle. Kenya's diverse landscapes, from the savannahs of the Maasai Mara to the highlands of Mount Kenya, add to its appeal. English and Swahili are widely spoken, easing communication for newcomers. **Ghana** is known for its stable democracy, rich history, and welcoming culture, making it a hub for African diasporans looking to reconnect with their heritage.

Accra, the capital, is a fast-developing city with vibrant nightlife, business opportunities, and a growing creative scene. The country's Right of Abode and Year of Return initiatives have made it a favored destination for those seeking to invest and build new lives in Africa. **South Africa** offers sophisticated infrastructure, a thriving economy, and breathtaking natural scenery, combining first-world amenities with cultural diversity. Johannesburg is ideal for business and industry professionals, while Cape Town attracts creatives and entrepreneurs drawn to its scenic coastline and vibrant arts scene. However, income inequality and crime remain concerns that require vigilance.

For those seeking a blend of adventure and serenity, **Tanzania** stands out. Home to Mount Kilimanjaro, the Serengeti, and Zanzibar's white sandy beaches, Tanzania is a haven for nature lovers. With a lower cost of living and a peaceful political climate, it offers an appealing lifestyle. Dar es Salaam is the commercial hub, while Arusha is popular among expatriates seeking a quieter life with easy access to national parks. **Nigeria,**

Africa's most populous nation and its largest economy, is a land of immense opportunity, particularly for entrepreneurs in tech, finance, and entertainment. Lagos, a fast-paced megacity, is the heart of the country's economic and cultural activity. While infrastructure challenges and congestion can be daunting, Nigeria's business environment is one of the most dynamic in Africa. **Namibia** is ideal for those seeking a tranquil, well-organized society with stunning landscapes. Windhoek, the capital, is clean, safe, and efficiently run, while the Namib Desert and Etosha National Park offer some of the most breathtaking natural scenery on the continent. With a small population and low crime rates, Namibia provides a high quality of life for those who value space and serenity.

Botswana is another standout destination, known for its stable government and strong economy. Gaborone, the capital, is modern and growing, offering a secure and business-friendly environment. The country's conservation efforts have also made it a premier location for ecotourism and wildlife enthusiasts. **Zambia**, an emerging relocation destination, offers a friendly and peaceful environment. Lusaka, the capital, is experiencing rapid development, and the country's business climate is gradually improving. Zambia is home to **Mosi-oa-Tunya** (formerly Victoria Falls), one of the world's greatest natural wonders, making it an attractive choice for those who appreciate nature and outdoor activities.

Language plays a crucial role in social and professional integration. While English, French, and Portuguese serve as official languages in many African nations, indigenous languages are still widely spoken. In countries like Tanzania and Kenya, Swahili is essential for day-to-day interactions, while in Ghana and Nigeria, Pidgin English can be beneficial for deeper cultural engagement. Understanding local languages can ease communication and enhance the relocation experience.

A key decision for any prospective mover is whether to settle in an urban or rural area. Africa's urban centers and rural communities offer vastly different experiences. **Urban Living** in cities such as Nairobi, Lagos, and Johannesburg provides modern conveniences, diverse social scenes, and business opportunities, but also comes with challenges like traffic congestion and a higher cost of living. **Rural Living** offers a slower pace, lower expenses, and stronger community ties, but may come with limitations in infrastructure, healthcare, and educational facilities. Weighing these pros and cons is essential when determining the best fit for your lifestyle and aspirations.

Navigating visa and residency policies is another crucial step in relocation. Some countries offer visa-free or visa-on-arrival options for certain passport holders, while others require extensive documentation. For long-term residency, common pathways include **Work and Business Visas**, which allow professionals and entrepreneurs to live and work legally. **Retirement Visas** cater to retirees with stable incomes, as seen in South Africa and Mauritius. **Repatriation Programs**, such as Ghana's Right of Abode and Rwanda's open-door policy for diasporans, provide unique opportunities for those of African descent to reconnect with their roots. Understanding these requirements will help ensure a smooth transition to life in Africa.

Selecting the right African country to relocate to requires careful analysis of various factors, from economic prospects to lifestyle preferences. While we have highlighted some of the most popular destinations based on feedback from our audience, Africa offers many more incredible places to explore. By understanding key considerations and exploring the unique offerings of different nations, you can make a well-informed choice that aligns with your personal and professional aspirations.

CHAPTER THREE

CITIZENSHIP & RESIDENCY PATHWAYS

"Restless feet might walk you into a snake pit" is a cautionary African proverb that warns against rushing into new situations without proper preparation. It suggests that impatience and lack of foresight can lead to unexpected dangers or hardships. Just as wandering aimlessly in unfamiliar terrain increases the risk of stepping into danger, making impulsive life decisions—such as relocating to a new country without adequate research—can result in unforeseen challenges. The proverb encourages thoughtfulness, careful planning, and a strategic approach to any major transition to ensure a successful and secure outcome.

Relocating to Africa requires meticulous planning, both in terms of financial stability and legal status. Understanding the economic landscape, cost of living, banking infrastructure, and pathways to citizenship or residency is crucial for anyone considering a long-term move. While Africa consists of 54 unique and vibrant nations, this chapter will focus on countries that have emerged as the most popular among our audience based on interest and surveys: Kenya, Ghana, South Africa, Tanzania, Nigeria, Namibia, Botswana, and Zambia. These nations offer a combination of economic opportunity, cultural richness, and various pathways for legal residency and citizenship. However, it is essential to recognize that Africa's diversity extends far beyond these highlighted destinations, and there are still numerous other incredible places to discover.

Pathways to Citizenship & Residency

For individuals looking to establish themselves legally in Africa, there are multiple pathways to gaining residency or even full citizenship. These options range from naturalization and investment programs to special repatriation initiatives designed to welcome African descendants back to the continent. Each country has its own set of regulations, and understanding these pathways can make the process smoother and more predictable.

Dual Citizenship & Naturalization

Many African countries allow dual citizenship, making it easier for foreigners to retain their original nationality while becoming a citizen of their new home. Ghana, for example, has an established dual citizenship framework that allows individuals of Ghanaian descent to reclaim their heritage legally while maintaining their original citizenship. South Africa also permits dual nationality, provided that citizens obtain permission from the government before acquiring a second passport. In contrast, countries like Namibia and Botswana are stricter, generally requiring individuals to renounce their previous citizenship before naturalization. Naturalization requirements typically include long-term residency, demonstrating financial independence, and cultural integration, such as proficiency in the local language or contributing to the country's economic or social development.

Repatriation Programs

Some African nations have launched programs specifically aimed at members of the African diaspora looking to return to their ancestral homeland. Ghana's **Right of Abode** program and the well-known **Year of Return** campaign have welcomed thousands of African Americans and other descendants of the transatlantic slave trade. These programs provide easier pathways to residency and citizenship, including the ability to acquire a Ghanaian passport without the need for extensive residency requirements. Similarly, Sierra Leone has granted citizenship to African descendants who can prove their lineage through DNA testing, setting a precedent for other nations to follow.

Investment & Business-Based Residency

Several African countries offer residency to individuals who invest in the local economy, whether through real estate, business ventures, or government bonds. In Kenya, individuals investing at least $100,000 in a business can qualify for a **Class G Investor Visa**, which allows them to reside in the country long-term. In South Africa, the **Independent Financial Permit** grants residency to individuals with significant net worth, typically requiring a minimum investment of around $300,000. Nigeria also offers business-based residency options, though the bureaucratic process can be challenging and often requires legal assistance to navigate. These investment programs are designed to attract foreign capital and skilled professionals, providing an opportunity for long-term economic contribution in exchange for legal status.

Long-Term Visas & Work Permits

For those looking for flexible residency without immediate citizenship, long-term visas and work permits provide viable alternatives. Tanzania offers a **Class B Work Permit** for skilled professionals employed by Tanzanian businesses, while Namibia has introduced digital nomad visas, allowing remote workers to live in the country for an extended period without traditional employment ties. Botswana and Zambia also offer work and residence permits for expatriates contributing to their workforce, although these typically require company sponsorship. Retirees looking for peaceful and affordable living options can apply for retirement visas in countries like South Africa and Kenya, which have established pathways catering to foreign retirees seeking stability and comfort.

Financial Considerations: Cost of Living & Budgeting

Financial planning is a critical component of relocating to Africa, as costs can vary widely depending on lifestyle preferences, location, and economic factors. While it is possible to live modestly in many parts of the continent, those seeking a high standard of living should budget accordingly. The cost of living in major cities like Lagos, Nairobi, Cape Town, and Accra is significantly higher than in rural areas or smaller towns.

Housing Costs

Housing is typically the most significant expense for expatriates and returnees. In Lagos, Nigeria's economic hub, a one-bedroom apartment in prime areas like Victoria Island or Ikoyi can range from **$1,500 to $3,000 per month,** while more affordable options in mainland areas such as Yaba or Surulere start around **$500 to $1,000 per month**. In Accra, Ghana, housing in sought-after neighborhoods like Cantonments and Labone averages **$800 to $1,500 per month**, whereas areas outside the city center offer rentals for as low as **$400 to $700**. Nairobi's prime locations such as Westlands and Kilimani offer apartments ranging from **$700 to $1,500 per month**, while South Africa's Cape Town and Johannesburg have premium rentals starting at **$1,200 to $2,500 per month**.

Those seeking a more rural lifestyle or traditional housing can find options for as low as **$500 per month** in most countries, though this typically comes with fewer modern conveniences. A realistic monthly housing budget for a comfortable lifestyle in a well-located neighborhood is between **$1,500 and $2,500** in major urban areas.

Day-to-Day Expenses: Groceries, Transportation & Utilities

Grocery prices vary depending on reliance on local versus imported goods. South Africa and Kenya offer relatively affordable food prices, with fresh produce being significantly cheaper than in the United States or Europe. Monthly grocery expenses for a single person in Nairobi typically range from **$200 to $300**, while in Lagos, the cost can be **$250 to $400**, depending on dietary habits. Transportation costs are also important to consider, as public transit varies in affordability and efficiency. A one-way bus ticket in Lagos costs around **$1**, while in Cape Town, it's approximately **$1.50**. Fuel prices fluctuate, particularly in oil-producing countries like Nigeria, where subsidy removals have recently impacted costs. Monthly utilities, including electricity, water, and internet, can range from **$100 to $250**, depending on location and consumption.

Banking & Money Transfers

Establishing a solid banking foundation is essential for managing finances in a new country. Major banks in Kenya, Ghana, South Africa, and Nigeria offer expat-friendly services, including USD-denominated accounts, investment options, and online banking. Mobile money platforms like **M-Pesa in Kenya**, **MTN Mobile Money in Ghana**, and **Paga in Nigeria** provide convenient ways to transfer funds and pay for services without needing traditional bank accounts. However, it is crucial to factor in currency exchange rates and transfer fees, as moving money internationally can be costly. Many expatriates find it beneficial to maintain accounts in both their home country and their new country of residence for financial flexibility.

Conclusion

Moving to Africa is an exciting and rewarding endeavor, but it requires thorough planning. Understanding the financial implications and legal pathways available can make the transition significantly smoother. Whether seeking dual citizenship, investment residency, or long-term visas, the opportunities in Africa are diverse. Budgeting appropriately for housing, day-to-day expenses, and banking considerations ensures financial stability, allowing for a fulfilling experience. As more people explore the possibility of living and working on the continent, having a clear financial and legal roadmap will be invaluable in making the most of the opportunities Africa has to offer.

CHAPTER FOUR

FINANCIAL PLANNING & BUILDING WEALTH IN AFRICA

"Tomorrow belongs to people who prepare for it today" *encapsulates the idea that future success and opportunities are shaped by the actions you take in the present. In the context of this book, it emphasizes the critical importance of thorough preparation—whether you're planning to relocate, invest, or immerse yourself in the culture of Africa. By laying a solid foundation now, you set the stage for a smoother, more rewarding transition to living The African Dream, ensuring that you are ready to seize the opportunities and overcome challenges that lie ahead.*

Managing finances effectively is crucial to thriving in Africa, particularly in key countries such as Nigeria, Kenya, South Africa, Ghana, Zambia, Namibia, Botswana, and Tanzania. Each of these countries presents unique opportunities and challenges that require strategic financial planning to maximize wealth-building potential. This chapter delves into budgeting for daily expenses, navigating the banking and financial systems, exploring investment opportunities, and managing risks to ensure long-term financial success in these diverse African nations.

Cost of Living – Budgeting for Housing, Transportation, Food, and Healthcare

The cost of living in Africa varies greatly from one country to another, depending on urbanization, regional economic development, and local market conditions. In cities like Lagos (Nigeria) and Nairobi (Kenya), housing costs can be significant, particularly in central areas where demand for rental properties is high. In contrast, cities like Lusaka (Zambia) and Dar es Salaam (Tanzania) may offer more affordable housing options but still require careful budgeting due to inflation and fluctuating property values.

Transportation costs also vary across the continent. In South Africa and Botswana, public transportation is well-developed, but taxis or ridesharing services like Uber can become expensive, particularly in major urban centers like Johannesburg and Gaborone. Meanwhile, in Ghana and Tanzania, you might rely more on informal transport systems, such as tro-tros (shared minivans), which are more affordable but may be less comfortable and less reliable. Additionally, the cost of fuel fluctuates, which should be factored into transportation budgets, especially in Namibia and Zambia, where fuel prices are influenced by global market trends.

Food costs across these countries are also subject to local agricultural conditions and supply chains. In countries like Kenya and South Africa, local food markets are often well-stocked with fresh produce, but imported goods can drive up prices. For example, staple foods like rice and wheat may fluctuate in price depending on local production or global supply chains. Healthcare costs also differ widely. South Africa offers a well-developed private healthcare sector, though private insurance can be expensive. In contrast, healthcare systems in countries like Ghana and Zambia may be more affordable but may require supplemental private insurance for high-quality care.

Banking & Money Transfers – Setting Up Local Accounts, Mobile Money, and International Transfers

Banking and money management in Africa are diverse, with varying levels of access and options available depending on the country. In South Africa, the banking system is highly developed, with access to both local and international banking services. Setting up a local account in cities like Cape Town and Johannesburg is straightforward, with banks offering robust digital banking services, including mobile apps for easy access to your funds. In contrast, countries like Zambia and Tanzania may have smaller banking networks, but they are growing rapidly as digital banking becomes more accessible.

Mobile money has transformed financial inclusion across Africa, particularly in countries like Kenya, Ghana, and Tanzania, where services such as M-Pesa and Tigo Pesa have expanded access to financial services for millions. These platforms allow users to send money, pay bills, and even access loans using only their mobile phones. In Ghana and Tanzania, mobile money services are especially popular in rural areas where traditional banking infrastructure is lacking. In countries like Nigeria and Botswana, mobile money is gaining momentum, providing an alternative to traditional banking for the unbanked population.

When it comes to international money transfers, African countries are increasingly connected to global remittance networks. In Kenya, Nigeria, and South Africa, remittance services like Western Union, WorldRemit, and TransferWise offer fast, affordable ways to send and receive money internationally. However, each country has its own regulations regarding cross-border transfers, so it is important to familiarize yourself with the best options for transferring funds, especially if you are frequently sending or receiving money across borders.

Investment Opportunities – Key Sectors to Invest In (Real Estate, Agriculture, Tourism, Tech, and More)

Africa presents diverse and exciting opportunities for investment, particularly in the sectors of real estate, agriculture, tourism, and technology. Real estate investment has seen significant growth in countries like Nigeria, Kenya, and South Africa. In Nigeria's commercial hub, Lagos, demand for residential and office spaces is rising, particularly in areas like Lekki and Victoria Island. Similarly, Nairobi's rapidly expanding skyline offers a wealth of opportunities in both residential and commercial property development. In countries like Ghana and Tanzania, real estate markets are also expanding as middle-class populations grow, creating demand for both residential and retail spaces.

Agriculture remains the backbone of many African economies, offering immense opportunities for agribusiness investment. In Zambia, with its rich agricultural land, sectors like crop production, livestock, and agro-processing are key areas of interest. In Namibia, agriculture is vital for food security, while in Ghana, cocoa farming and agro-processing businesses are lucrative sectors for investment. The tourism sector also presents attractive opportunities, particularly in South Africa, Kenya, and Botswana. These countries are known for their diverse landscapes, wildlife, and cultural heritage, making them popular tourist destinations. Investing in eco-tourism, safari lodges, and hospitality ventures is an increasingly popular choice in these regions.

The tech sector is one of the fastest-growing industries in Africa, with countries like Kenya, Nigeria, and South Africa emerging as technology hubs. In Kenya's "Silicon Savannah," the startup ecosystem is thriving, particularly in fintech and e-commerce. In Nigeria, Lagos is home to a burgeoning tech scene, with investors flocking to fund innovative startups in areas such as fintech, mobile applications, and digital services. South Africa, too, is experiencing growth in the tech space, with opportunities in mobile technology, e-commerce, and renewable energy.

Entrepreneurship in Africa – Starting and Growing a Business

Entrepreneurship is a key driver of economic growth across Africa. The continent is home to a rapidly growing pool of young entrepreneurs who are capitalizing on new technologies, solving local problems, and creating wealth. In Nigeria, the thriving tech and entertainment industries offer entrepreneurs an opportunity to tap into lucrative markets. The same is true for Kenya, where innovation in agriculture, fintech, and mobile services is driving a new wave of entrepreneurial activity.

In South Africa, small and medium-sized enterprises (SMEs) are integral to the economy, and many entrepreneurs are finding success in areas like fashion, food services, and digital marketing. Countries like Botswana and Namibia provide a more stable environment for new businesses, offering opportunities in sectors such as mining, tourism, and real estate. For entrepreneurs in Ghana, government initiatives like the National Entrepreneurship and Innovation Plan (NEIP) provide financial support and resources to help businesses grow.

Starting a business in Africa requires a deep understanding of the local market, navigating regulatory frameworks, and building strong networks. In Zambia, local businesses benefit from a supportive entrepreneurial ecosystem that encourages foreign investment and partnerships. Meanwhile, Tanzania has seen significant growth in small businesses, particularly in the tech and retail sectors, due to supportive government policies and initiatives that help entrepreneurs access finance and markets.

Managing Risks – Protecting Assets and Navigating Economic Fluctuations

Africa's economic landscape can be volatile, with factors such as inflation, currency fluctuations, and political instability affecting business operations and investment returns. In countries like Nigeria, Zambia, and South Africa, inflation rates can fluctuate, leading to unexpected increases in the cost of living and operational costs for businesses. Currency devaluation is another risk, as seen in the Nigerian Naira and the Zambian Kwacha, which can impact foreign investments and profits.

Managing risk in Africa involves diversifying investments, obtaining insurance, and staying informed about local economic conditions. For example, diversifying into real estate, stocks, agriculture, and government bonds can help mitigate the risks of economic instability. In Botswana, Namibia, and South Africa, strong insurance markets provide options for protecting assets, whether personal or business-related. In countries like Ghana and Tanzania, the risks are often lower due to political stability, but it is still important to monitor market conditions and adjust financial plans accordingly.

To successfully protect your assets and investments, it's essential to build an adaptive strategy that includes diversifying income sources, ensuring insurance coverage, and staying connected with local business networks to keep up with regulatory changes and economic trends. By understanding these risks and taking proactive steps to mitigate them, you can protect and grow your wealth in Africa.

CHAPTER FIVE

FINDING HOUSING & SETTLING IN

"No shortcuts exist to the top of a palm tree" reminds us that finding a home, building, or settling in—much like reaching the top of a palm tree—requires patient, step-by-step effort. There's no quick fix or easy route when it comes to establishing a secure and fulfilling place to live; each phase of the journey demands careful planning, perseverance, and dedication. This adage serves as a powerful reminder that the stability and comfort of a true home are achieved only through diligent work and commitment over time.

Finding and securing a home is one of the most critical aspects of settling into any new country, and when moving to Africa, this process can come with unique challenges and opportunities. Understanding the nuances of the local housing market, negotiating rental agreements, building a home, and setting up essential services and utilities can significantly impact your overall experience. Whether you're looking to rent, buy, or build, this chapter offers practical guidance for navigating housing in some of Africa's most dynamic countries, including Nigeria, Kenya, South Africa, Ghana, Zambia, Namibia, Botswana, and Tanzania. We'll break down how to approach these issues in a way that ensures you're well-prepared for your move and settlement.

When relocating to Africa, one of the first decisions you'll need to make is whether to rent or buy property. Each option comes with its benefits and challenges, and your decision will largely depend on your long-term plans, financial situation, and the country you are moving to. Renting property is a flexible and relatively low-risk option, especially if you're unsure of how long you'll be staying in a particular country or city. It allows you to adjust your living situation as needed, making it a good option for expatriates or those in transitional stages. Renting typically requires lower upfront costs, such as a deposit and a few months' rent in advance, compared to the large financial outlay required when buying.

Additionally, renting means that the responsibility for repairs and maintenance usually falls on the landlord, sparing you the burden of costly upkeep. However, renting comes with its own challenges, such as the fact that you're not building equity, and rent payments are ongoing with no return on investment. In some regions, especially in countries like Nigeria and Ghana, the housing market is also susceptible to scams, with fraudulent landlords attempting to take advantage of newcomers. It's essential to verify the legitimacy of rental properties through reliable real estate agents or trusted local contacts and never pay upfront without seeing the property in person.

On the other hand, buying property in Africa can be a solid long-term investment, particularly in cities like Lagos, Nairobi, Cape Town, and Accra, where property values are increasing due to growing populations and urbanization. Owning a property allows you to build equity, and the value of your home may appreciate over time, giving you a potential return on your investment. Homeownership also provides long-term stability, meaning you're not subject to sudden rent hikes or the potential instability of the rental market.

In some countries, such as South Africa, Nigeria, and Kenya, owning property can also allow you to generate income by renting out your property. However, the process of buying property in Africa comes with significant challenges. The initial costs are high, and securing a mortgage can be a complex process depending on the country's financial systems. In addition, real estate markets in some countries, such as Nigeria, are unpredictable, and land titles may not always be clear, especially in rural areas. It's important to exercise due diligence when purchasing property and work with trusted professionals to avoid common pitfalls, such as property fraud or ambiguous land ownership issues.

The real estate market in Africa can vary widely depending on the region and country, with each location offering distinct housing trends and challenges. In South Africa, for example, cities like Johannesburg, Cape Town, and Pretoria have well-established real estate markets. These urban areas offer a wide range of housing options, from luxury apartments in Sandton to suburban family homes in Cape Town. However, these properties tend to come with high prices, particularly in central business districts or affluent neighborhoods. In Johannesburg, a 1-bedroom apartment in the city center can cost between ZAR 7,000 to ZAR 15,000 per month, and many properties are located in gated communities with 24/7 security due to safety concerns in urban areas.

South Africa's real estate market is generally stable but can be influenced by economic fluctuations and political factors, making it important to keep an eye on market trends. In Nigeria, particularly in Lagos, Abuja, and Port Harcourt, the real estate market is growing rapidly due to the increasing population and demand for housing. However, Nigeria's market is prone to volatility, and fraud is common, especially in Lagos. Renting a 2-bedroom apartment in Lagos can cost anywhere from NGN 500,000 to NGN 3,000,000 per year, depending on the location. Property ownership laws in Nigeria are also complex, and verifying the legitimacy of land titles through government agencies or legal advisors is crucial. Similarly, Kenya's real estate market in Nairobi is experiencing significant growth, and the city is home to many modern, well-developed neighborhoods. Rental costs in Nairobi for a 1-bedroom apartment can range from KES 50,000 to KES 150,000 per month, depending on the area and amenities. The market is still maturing, but it presents great opportunities for investment, particularly for expatriates and professionals seeking modern living spaces in a rapidly growing city.

In Ghana, the real estate market is booming, particularly in Accra, which has seen an influx of both local and international investors. Accra offers a wide variety of housing options, from affordable apartments to high-end, luxury residences in areas like East Legon and Cantonments. Renting a 2-bedroom apartment in Accra typically costs between GHS 1,500 and GHS 5,000 per month, depending on the location and amenities. While Ghana offers relatively affordable housing compared to South Africa or Nigeria, the country's property laws can be complicated. In some areas, customary land ownership laws may apply, making it necessary to work with a lawyer to ensure that the land is properly titled. In countries like Zambia, Namibia, Botswana, and Tanzania, real estate markets are emerging and less competitive than in the larger economies. These nations offer a range of affordable housing options, especially in their capital cities, and present opportunities for both personal homeownership and investment, particularly in tourist or industrial areas. In Lusaka, Zambia, a 2-bedroom apartment can rent for ZMW 5,000 to ZMW 12,000 per month, while in Gaborone, Botswana, and Windhoek, Namibia, rental prices are relatively moderate, reflecting a slower-paced but steady market growth.

Once you've decided whether to rent or buy, understanding how to negotiate lease agreements is essential for avoiding misunderstandings and ensuring that you're legally protected. Rental agreements in African countries can differ widely, so it's important to fully understand the terms before committing. In most African countries, rental leases typically range from 6 months to one year, and it's common for landlords to ask for a deposit and advance payment, sometimes as much as one year of rent upfront. When reviewing a lease agreement, ensure that it clearly specifies the duration of the lease, rent payment terms (whether monthly, quarterly, or annually), and who is responsible for maintenance and repairs. It's also crucial to check if utilities like electricity, water, and internet are included in the rent, as this varies from country to country and property to property. Pay particular attention to the termination clause, which will specify how much notice you need to give before vacating the property. This is especially important in countries like South Africa, where lease agreements are tightly regulated, and tenants have specific rights. In many African countries, landlords may not be as transparent as in Western markets, so always ensure the lease is reviewed by a local legal expert.

For those who are looking to build a home rather than renting or buying an existing property, the process of purchasing land and constructing a house in Africa involves several important steps. First, verifying land ownership is crucial, particularly in countries like Ghana, Kenya, and Tanzania, where customary land ownership laws may complicate the legal process. It's important to conduct thorough research and work with a lawyer to confirm the land's ownership status through official channels, such as the Land Registry or the Ministry of Lands. After securing the land, you'll need to obtain the necessary building permits and approvals from local authorities, which may require submitting architectural plans and complying with zoning laws. The construction process can take anywhere from several months to years, depending on the complexity of the project and availability of materials. In more developed countries like South Africa, the construction process is relatively straightforward, but in countries like Zambia or Tanzania, you may need to rely on local contractors or builders. Regardless of the location, ensuring that all permits are in order and working with a reputable construction company will help streamline the process. After building the house, connecting essential services such as water, electricity, and internet is the next step. In urban areas, these services are usually readily available, but in rural areas, you may need to explore alternatives such as solar energy or boreholes for water.

Lastly, setting up essential services and utilities is a critical part of settling into your new home. Depending on the country, access to services like water, electricity, and internet can vary. In South Africa and Kenya, water is typically supplied by municipal authorities, though in rural areas, you may need to consider alternatives such as boreholes or rainwater harvesting. Electricity supply can also be an issue in countries like South Africa, where load shedding and power outages are common. In these cases, it may be wise to invest in a backup generator or explore renewable energy options like solar panels. In larger cities like Nairobi, Accra, and Lagos, internet and mobile services are widely available, and fiber-optic internet is becoming more common. However, in rural regions, mobile data may be your most reliable option, although speeds may be slower. Security is another essential aspect of settling in, particularly in urban areas where crime rates can be higher. Many cities in Africa, such as Johannesburg, Lagos, and Nairobi, have high-security expectations, and it's common for homes to have private security services, gated communities, and surveillance systems. Whether renting or owning, installing security systems like alarm systems, burglar bars, and motion detectors can provide peace of mind.

In conclusion, whether you are renting, buying, or building a home in Africa, it's essential to thoroughly research local markets, understand your rights as a tenant or homeowner, and be prepared for the logistical challenges of settling into a new country. Take your time to carefully consider the housing options available, negotiate lease agreements, verify property ownership, and set up essential services to ensure that your new home provides a comfortable and secure living environment. By approaching the housing process with patience, diligence, and awareness of the local context, you can lay a strong foundation for a successful and fulfilling life in Africa.

CHAPTER SIX

BUSINESS & EMPLOYMENT OPPORTUNITIES

"If you are filled with pride, then you will have no room for wisdom" *means that excessive self-importance can obstruct your ability to learn, grow, and gain insight. When pride dominates, it blinds you to new perspectives, constructive feedback, and the humility necessary to admit mistakes. Wisdom is cultivated through openness and self-awareness, qualities that flourish only when pride is kept in check.*

Africa is a land of vast economic opportunities, with growing markets, emerging industries, and a youthful workforce. Whether you're a professional seeking employment, an entrepreneur looking to start a business, or an investor searching for promising ventures, understanding the job market and business environment is essential for success. Each country within our focus—Kenya, Ghana, Tanzania, Zambia, Nigeria, South Africa, Namibia, and Botswana—has its own economic strengths, challenges, and regulatory landscapes. This chapter provides an in-depth guide on navigating Africa's professional landscape with practical strategies for finding employment, launching a business, networking, overcoming challenges, and leveraging side hustles to build sustainable income streams.

While employment remains an option, business and entrepreneurship offer far greater opportunities in Africa. Job seekers often face challenges due to limited formal employment opportunities, high competition, and slower career progression in certain industries. However, those with international experience, strong educational backgrounds, technical skills, and a global mindset often find an advantage in sectors such as banking, engineering, ICT, healthcare, and consulting. Employers value customer service expertise, understanding of global standards, and the ability to navigate cross-cultural work environments. Professionals with Western work experience or certifications in fields such as project management, software development, finance, and logistics are particularly sought after. Nonetheless, job seekers must be prepared for a highly competitive market where networking, professional development, and personal branding play a crucial role in securing opportunities.

The job market in Africa varies significantly from country to country, with certain industries offering more opportunities than others. In Kenya, the technology sector, often referred to as "Silicon Savannah," is booming, with fintech, mobile banking, and e-commerce leading the way. Ghana has a strong presence in oil and gas, mining, and telecommunications, offering competitive job prospects for professionals in these sectors. Tanzania's tourism industry, agriculture, and mining provide lucrative employment opportunities, while Zambia's economy is driven by copper mining, agriculture, and financial services. Nigeria's job market is heavily influenced by fintech, the booming entertainment industry (Nollywood and Afrobeats), e-commerce, and agriculture. South Africa's well-developed economy has strong banking, telecommunications, energy, and manufacturing sectors, while Namibia thrives on mining, tourism, and logistics. Botswana, known for its political stability and well-managed economy, presents job opportunities in diamond mining, financial services, and eco-tourism. Professionals seeking employment should explore opportunities on job portals such as BrighterMonday (Kenya, Ghana), MyJobMag (Nigeria, Zambia), and Career Junction (South Africa), as well as through networking events, LinkedIn communities, and recruitment agencies that specialize in African markets.

However, the greatest potential for financial success lies in entrepreneurship. Africa is still developing across many industries, which presents an abundance of opportunities for those willing to take the risk and create businesses. The demand for infrastructure, services, technology, and manufacturing is immense, meaning that entrepreneurs who can solve problems, provide innovative solutions, or meet consumer needs have the potential for high rewards. Unlike employment, where income is often capped and career progression slow, business ownership allows individuals to build generational wealth, expand into new markets, and contribute to job creation. While starting a business carries high risks, the upside is far greater, as Africa is in a phase of rapid economic transformation with massive opportunities in construction, energy, healthcare, logistics, and digital services.

For those looking to start a business, Africa offers fertile ground for entrepreneurship, with many governments actively supporting startups and small businesses through incentives and funding programs. However, understanding the business registration process and legal requirements in each country is crucial. In Kenya, business registration is done through the eCitizen portal, while Ghana requires registration with the Registrar General's Department and compliance with the Ghana Revenue Authority. Tanzania's registration is managed via BRELA, with sector-specific licensing requirements. Zambia's businesses must register with PACRA and obtain tax clearance from ZRA. In Nigeria, registration with the Corporate Affairs Commission (CAC) is mandatory, alongside regulatory approvals depending on the industry. South Africa requires businesses to register with the Companies and Intellectual Property Commission (CIPC) and comply with Broad-Based Black Economic Empowerment (BEE) regulations. Namibia's business registration is handled by BIPA, and Botswana requires compliance with CIPA. Entrepreneurs must also explore funding options such as government grants, venture capital, bank loans, and alternative financing models like crowdfunding. Kenya and Nigeria, in particular, have robust startup ecosystems, while microfinance institutions in Tanzania, Zambia, and Namibia offer essential support for small business owners.

Networking plays a crucial role in business and career advancement. Professionals and entrepreneurs should engage with industry associations, chambers of commerce, and business networking groups to connect with potential partners, clients, and investors. Organizations such as the Kenya National Chamber of Commerce, Ghana Investment Promotion Centre, and South African Chamber of Commerce offer invaluable networking opportunities. Additionally, co-working spaces and innovation hubs like Nairobi Garage (Kenya), Impact Hub (Ghana), and BongoHive (Zambia) provide platforms for collaboration and mentorship. Online communities on LinkedIn and sector-specific professional groups can also be useful in establishing business connections and finding job leads. Attending industry conferences, expos, and startup incubator events further enhances opportunities for growth and visibility within Africa's business ecosystem.

While Africa presents immense opportunities, doing business or securing employment comes with its own set of challenges. Bureaucratic red tape can slow down business registration processes, requiring entrepreneurs to seek legal consultants or use government e-services to streamline compliance. Limited access to funding is another significant hurdle, which can be addressed by tapping into venture capital networks, diaspora investment programs, and microfinance institutions. Market competition is fierce, making thorough market research and a strong digital marketing strategy essential for business success. Infrastructure gaps, such as inconsistent power supply and limited broadband internet in some regions, require businesses to invest in backup power solutions and alternative communication technologies. Additionally, the shortage of skilled labor in certain industries highlights the importance of investing in employee training and development programs to build a competitive workforce.

For those looking to generate income outside traditional employment, the digital economy and gig work present exciting possibilities. Freelancing opportunities in writing, graphic design, and programming are in high demand on platforms such as Upwork and Fiverr. E-commerce businesses, including dropshipping, print-on-demand, and selling through local online marketplaces, have significant profit potential. The rise of digital marketing and content creation also provides monetization opportunities through YouTube, blogging, and social media influencing. Agriculture-based side businesses, such as small-scale farming and organic food production, are viable in rural areas with access to fertile land. With remote work becoming increasingly viable, many professionals are capitalizing on the ability to work with international clients while residing in Africa, leveraging lower living costs to maximize earnings.

Africa's economic landscape is full of opportunities for job seekers, entrepreneurs, and investors willing to navigate the challenges and harness the potential of emerging industries. However, the best path to financial independence and long-term success remains business ownership. Creating jobs is the highest-risk but highest-reward venture, as it allows entrepreneurs to tap into Africa's rapid development and infrastructure growth. Whether one's goal is to secure high-paying employment, establish a thriving business, or explore new income streams through freelancing and digital ventures, Africa provides a wealth of possibilities. The key to success lies in resilience, continuous learning, and strategic planning to unlock the continent's full economic potential.

CHAPTER SEVEN

HEALTHCARE, SAFETY & WELLNESS

"If you want to know the end, look at the beginning" suggests that the outcome of a situation is often determined by its origins, foundations, or the initial steps taken. It emphasizes the importance of understanding the roots, decisions, or actions at the start of a journey or process, as these often set the trajectory for how things will unfold.

Moving to a new country comes with the responsibility of ensuring your health, safety, and overall well-being. Access to quality healthcare, understanding local medical practices, and taking preventive measures are critical for a smooth transition. In Africa, healthcare systems vary significantly across different countries, with some nations offering robust private healthcare options while others require careful navigation of public services. Additionally, staying safe and maintaining mental and emotional well-being are key aspects of thriving in a new environment. This chapter provides practical guidance on healthcare, safety, and overall wellness in

Nigeria, Kenya, South Africa, Ghana, Zambia, Namibia, Botswana, and Tanzania.

Understanding the Healthcare System

Healthcare in Africa ranges from world-class private hospitals to underfunded public health facilities. In countries like South Africa and Kenya, private hospitals provide high-quality care comparable to Western standards, but costs can be high. Nigeria and Ghana have both public and private healthcare systems, with private hospitals being the preferred option for quality care. Botswana and Namibia offer relatively strong public healthcare systems but still have gaps in specialized care. Zambia and Tanzania have improving healthcare infrastructures, but private healthcare is generally the better option for more serious medical needs. It is essential to research and locate reputable hospitals, clinics, and pharmacies before arriving in your chosen destination. Many expatriates and returning diaspora members opt for private healthcare due to better services, shorter wait times, and access to specialized medical practitioners.

Health Insurance & Medical Costs

Health insurance is crucial for managing medical costs in Africa, as out-of-pocket expenses for private healthcare can be high. Countries like South Africa,

Kenya, and Ghana have local insurance providers that offer comprehensive health plans, but international health insurance may be a better choice for those seeking coverage across multiple countries. Nigeria and Zambia have emerging health insurance markets, with government and private schemes providing different levels of coverage. In Botswana and Namibia, residents have access to national health insurance schemes, but expats often prefer international plans for more extensive coverage. It is important to compare insurance plans based on coverage, network hospitals, and reimbursement policies. Additionally, medical costs vary, with urban centers offering better healthcare facilities than rural areas, where access to specialized care may be limited.

Vaccinations & Preventative Care

Before relocating, it is important to be up-to-date on essential vaccinations and preventive treatments. Vaccinations for yellow fever, hepatitis A and B, typhoid, meningitis, and polio are often recommended or required before entering African countries. Malaria is prevalent in many parts of Africa, including Nigeria, Ghana, Kenya, and Zambia, making antimalarial medication a necessity for travelers and new residents. In South Africa and Namibia, malaria risk is lower but still exists in certain regions. Preventative healthcare measures such as regular check-ups, a healthy diet, and access to clean water are important for maintaining overall wellness. It is advisable to register with a local doctor or clinic upon arrival and have a list of emergency contacts, including local hospitals, embassies, and medical evacuation services.

Safety & Security

Safety is a major consideration when moving to a new country, and understanding local security conditions is crucial. While many African nations are relatively safe, petty crimes such as pickpocketing, scams, and burglary can occur, particularly in major cities like Lagos, Nairobi, Johannesburg, and Accra. South Africa has higher crime rates in certain areas, requiring extra vigilance. Namibia, Botswana, and Zambia are generally safer, but it is still essential to exercise caution, especially in urban centers. Avoiding displaying wealth, using trusted transportation services, and staying informed about local crime trends can help mitigate risks. Additionally, understanding local laws and law enforcement procedures is important for avoiding legal trouble. Establishing relationships with local communities and expatriate networks can provide additional safety insights and support.

Mental & Emotional Well-Being

Relocating to a new country can be an exciting yet overwhelming experience, and mental well-being should not be overlooked. Culture shock, homesickness, and the stress of adapting to a new environment can affect emotional health. Finding social support through local communities, religious groups, and expatriate networks can ease the transition. Many African countries, including Kenya, Ghana, and South Africa, have wellness centers, therapy services, and support groups that can help individuals cope with emotional challenges. Developing a routine, engaging in physical activities, and exploring local culture can also contribute to a sense of belonging. Additionally, maintaining communication with family and friends back home through digital platforms can provide emotional stability. Investing in self-care and seeking professional help when needed can ensure a smooth and fulfilling transition.

Healthcare, safety, and overall wellness are essential factors to consider when relocating to Africa. Understanding healthcare options, securing the right health insurance, taking preventive health measures, staying vigilant about safety, and prioritizing mental well-being can help ensure a positive experience. By taking proactive steps and staying informed, newcomers can navigate challenges effectively and enjoy a fulfilling and healthy life in their new home.

CHAPTER EIGHT

EDUCATION & RAISING A FAMILY IN AFRICA

"Knowledge is a garden. If it isn't cultivated, you can't harvest it" *means that knowledge, like a garden, requires consistent effort and care to grow and be useful. Simply acquiring knowledge isn't enough; it must be nurtured through practice, reflection, and application to yield benefits. Without active engagement and continuous growth, knowledge becomes stagnant and cannot lead to meaningful outcomes or success.*

Relocating to Africa with children is a transformative journey that requires thoughtful planning. The availability and quality of education, cost considerations, and cultural integration all play a role in ensuring a smooth transition for families. Each country in Africa has a distinct education system, influenced by its colonial history and local policies. Parents must evaluate their options based on curriculum, language of instruction, and affordability.

Nigeria's education system consists of public schools, private institutions, and a growing number of international schools. While public schools are the most affordable, they often suffer from underfunding, overcrowding, and inconsistent quality. Private schools, particularly in cities like Lagos and Abuja, offer better resources and a more structured curriculum. International schools following British, American, or IB curricula are popular among expatriates and diaspora families but come with higher tuition fees.

Ghana's education system is well-structured, with a growing emphasis on quality. Public schools follow the Ghanaian national curriculum, while private institutions, especially in Accra and Kumasi, offer high-quality education with modern facilities. International schools such as Lincoln Community School and Ghana International School cater to students seeking global curriculums.

Kenya has a robust mix of public, private, and international schools. The 8-4-4 education system is being phased out in favor of the Competency-Based Curriculum (CBC). Nairobi hosts some of the best private and international schools, such as Brookhouse and the International School of Kenya (ISK). Public schools vary in quality, but many parents opt for private alternatives.

South Africa has one of the most developed education systems on the continent, with a strong private and international school sector. Cape Town and Johannesburg are hubs for prestigious institutions, such as the American International School of Johannesburg. The government-funded Model C schools provide an affordable yet high-quality alternative to private education.

Tanzania's education system is improving, with Dar es Salaam and Arusha hosting some of the best private and international schools. The United World College and Haven of Peace Academy offer globally recognized curricula. Public schools teach primarily in Swahili, making private and international schools preferable for diaspora families.

Namibia's education sector is well-regulated, with public schools offering decent quality education, especially in urban areas. Windhoek hosts some of the best private schools, including St. Paul's College and Windhoek International School, which follow Cambridge and IB curricula.

Botswana's stable education system provides both public and private options. The country has well-funded government schools, while private institutions such as Maru-a-Pula School in Gaborone offer world-class education. Botswana's emphasis on bilingual education makes it an attractive destination for families.

Homeschooling is an option for parents seeking flexibility. While not common in most African countries, it is legally permitted in Kenya, South Africa, and Namibia. Parents in Nigeria and Ghana often form cooperative homeschooling networks, allowing children to engage in group learning while following international curriculums. Alternative education is also gaining popularity, with Montessori and Waldorf schools thriving in Kenya, Ghana, and South Africa. Afrocentric education programs in Nigeria and Tanzania incorporate African history and indigenous knowledge into learning, while hybrid learning models combining online education with community-based mentorship are emerging across Africa.

Education costs vary widely across the continent. Public schools are free or low-cost but may require additional expenses for books, uniforms, and extracurriculars. Private schools, depending on their reputation and facilities, can cost between $1,000 and $10,000 per year. International schools, particularly in cities like Lagos, Nairobi, and Johannesburg, have tuition fees ranging from $10,000 to over $30,000 per year. Parents should also budget for transportation, school meals, and extracurricular activities, which can significantly increase overall expenses.

African countries emphasize strong family and community ties, which provide an excellent support system for raising children. In Nigeria and Ghana, extended families play an active role in child-rearing, with a strong emphasis on respect and community. Kenya and Tanzania's cultural traditions and ceremonies offer children a sense of belonging, while South Africa and Namibia provide a blend of modern and traditional influences, allowing children to experience both African heritage and global perspectives. Botswana, known for its safety and political stability, is considered one of the best places to raise a family in Africa.

For diaspora children, balancing their heritage with their new African home is key to long-term integration. Language learning is crucial, and many private and international schools offer bilingual programs. Learning local languages such as Swahili in Kenya and Tanzania or Yoruba in Nigeria helps children connect deeply with their environment. Encouraging participation in cultural activities, sports, and local events strengthens their sense of belonging. Parents should also ensure their children remain connected to both their African roots and their diaspora culture to build a strong dual identity.

Raising a family in Africa offers immense opportunities for growth and cultural connection. By understanding the education system, planning finances, and embracing integration, families can successfully transition into their new home while contributing to Africa's future.

CHAPTER NINE

TRAVEL, EXPLORATION & ENJOYING AFRICAN CULTURE

*The phrase **"Once you carry your own water, you'll remember every drop"** means that experiencing the effort required to achieve or obtain something makes you value it more. It emphasizes the importance of personal responsibility and hard work, suggesting that when you directly handle a task or challenge, you develop a deeper appreciation for the resources, effort, or results involved.*

One of the greatest joys of living in Africa is immersing oneself in its rich cultures, breathtaking landscapes, and vibrant traditions. Each country has a unique identity shaped by history, geography, and its people, offering endless opportunities for exploration. Whether you seek adventure, relaxation, or cultural enrichment, Africa provides a dynamic and fulfilling lifestyle that blends tradition with modernity.

It is important to distinguish between **traveling with intent and being a tourist**. A tourist often experiences a country from the surface—visiting landmarks, staying in resorts, and enjoying planned excursions—while a traveler with intent seeks deeper engagement, understanding, and connection. Traveling with intent means exploring with the purpose of cultural exchange, learning, and building relationships. Those who choose to live in Africa should embrace the mindset of a traveler rather than a tourist, integrating into communities and respecting local customs while discovering the continent's vast offerings.

Africa consists of **54 countries and six regions**, as recognized by the African Union. The five continental regions include North, South, East, West, and Central Africa, with the **sixth region being the African diaspora**—those of African descent living outside the continent. Whether one chooses to explore North Africa's historical wonders, the wildlife-rich landscapes of Southern Africa, the cultural vibrancy of West Africa, the breathtaking terrains of East Africa, or the heartland of Central Africa, each region offers unique experiences. Most of the countries we feature in this book are concentrated within specific regions, and this context is important when planning travel, relocation, or business engagement.

Top Travel Destinations

Africa is home to some of the world's most stunning travel destinations. In **Nigeria**, Lagos stands out with its beaches, art galleries, and nightlife, while Calabar offers lush landscapes and the famous Calabar Carnival. **Ghana** attracts visitors with the historic Cape Coast Castle, the vibrant streets of Accra, and the serene beaches of Ada Foah. **Kenya** boasts the Maasai Mara, where the Great Migration occurs, alongside Nairobi's national park and Diani Beach's pristine coastline. **South Africa** is a paradise for explorers, offering Cape Town's Table Mountain, Johannesburg's rich history, and Kruger National Park's wildlife safaris. **Tanzania** is home to the breathtaking Serengeti, Mount Kilimanjaro, and Zanzibar's white-sand beaches. **Namibia** offers striking desert landscapes such as the towering dunes of Sossusvlei, and **Botswana** is world-famous for the Okavango Delta, a haven for wildlife enthusiasts. Whether you prefer the energy of bustling cities or the tranquility of nature, Africa has something for everyone.

Transportation & Getting Around

Navigating Africa requires understanding the various transportation options available. Most countries have well-connected airports, with Lagos, Accra, Nairobi, Johannesburg, and Cape Town serving as major international hubs. Domestic travel is facilitated by regional airlines such as Air Peace in Nigeria, Kenya

Airways, and South African Airways. Within cities, ride-hailing services like Bolt and Uber operate in urban areas, while minibus taxis, boda bodas (motorbike taxis), and tuk-tuks are common in countries like Kenya, Ghana, and Tanzania. Train travel is also an option in South Africa, with the Gautrain providing a reliable way to move between Johannesburg and Pretoria. Road trips are a great way to explore Namibia's vast deserts, Botswana's game reserves, and Ghana's coastal regions, but travelers should be mindful of road conditions and driving regulations in each country.

Social Life & Entertainment

Africa's social scene is vibrant and diverse. **Music** plays a central role, with Afrobeats dominating in Nigeria and Ghana, Amapiano setting the tone in South Africa and Botswana, and Bongo Flava defining Tanzania's nightlife. Nairobi, Lagos, and Johannesburg offer thriving entertainment districts with clubs, lounges, and live music venues. Cultural festivals such as Afrochella in Ghana, the Cape Town Jazz Festival in South Africa, and the Marula Festival in Botswana bring people together to celebrate art, music, and heritage. Kenya's Safari Rally and Tanzania's Serengeti Marathon offer exciting sporting events for adventure seekers. South Africa and Namibia have a booming wine tourism industry, with vineyard tours and tastings becoming popular weekend getaways.

Food & Culinary Experiences

Africa's culinary landscape is as diverse as its people. **Nigeria** is famous for jollof rice, suya, and pounded yam with egusi soup. In **Ghana**, waakye, fufu, and tilapia are local favorites. **Kenya** offers delicacies like nyama choma (grilled meat), ugali, and samosas, while **Tanzania** is known for its Swahili dishes, including pilau and mishkaki. **South Africa** boasts a fusion of African, Indian, and European flavors, with dishes such as bunny chow, bobotie, and braai (barbecue). **Namibia** serves game meats like oryx and kudu, while **Botswana** is known for seswaa, a slow-cooked beef dish. The street food scene is vibrant across all these countries, with local markets offering fresh and affordable meals that provide a true taste of the culture. Fine dining establishments in Nairobi, Lagos, and Cape Town also offer international cuisine for those seeking gourmet experiences.

Building Community

Integrating into local and expat communities is essential for a fulfilling experience in Africa. Many cities have thriving expatriate networks, particularly in Nairobi, Accra, and Johannesburg, where social clubs and networking events help newcomers establish connections. Diaspora communities often host cultural meetups, workshops, and business networking events to foster collaboration. Community engagement through volunteering, attending local festivals, and participating in traditional ceremonies helps deepen cultural understanding. Religious institutions, professional organizations, and hobby-based groups, such as hiking or photography clubs, provide avenues to build meaningful relationships. In African culture, relationships are valued, and building genuine connections with locals leads to an enriched experience and a true sense of belonging.

From the bustling streets of Lagos to the tranquil landscapes of Namibia, Africa offers a wealth of experiences that cater to every lifestyle. Whether you are an adventurer, foodie, music lover, or history enthusiast, the continent provides countless opportunities to explore, connect, and thrive. Embracing African culture and its diverse offerings ensures a rewarding and unforgettable journey for those who choose to call the continent home.

CHAPTER TEN

SUSTAINING THE AFRICAN DREAM

*The African proverb **"When the roots are deep, there is no reason to fear the wind"** metaphorically illustrates the significance of having strong and stable foundations in life. Deep roots symbolize the essential qualities, values, or structures that provide stability and strength, whether for an individual, a family, or a community. The wind represents challenges, adversities, and external pressures that can threaten to destabilize or uproot someone who is unprepared or lacks grounding.*

Relocating to Africa is not just about finding a new home—it is about fully immersing in a lifestyle that fosters growth, connection, and purpose. The African Dream is not merely a concept; it is a call to action, a movement towards a sustainable, fulfilling existence rooted in the principles of Afrocentric Regenerative Travel, conscious capitalism, and a true Pan-African way of life. Whether you have settled in Nigeria, Ghana, Tanzania, Namibia, Botswana, South Africa, or Kenya, your journey does not end with arrival. This chapter explores how to sustain and thrive in your new home while contributing to the broader mission of collective prosperity and cultural integration.

Building Wealth & Creating Legacy

Thriving in Africa requires strategic financial planning, wise investments, and a commitment to building long-term wealth. Many African economies offer lucrative opportunities in real estate, entrepreneurship, agriculture, and technology. Understanding local markets, legal frameworks, and business culture is key to making informed decisions. Conscious capitalism plays a vital role in economic success—not just generating profit, but doing so in a way that uplifts communities and sustains local ecosystems. Those embracing Afrocentric Regenerative Travel find ways to build wealth while reinvesting in the continent, supporting local businesses, and fostering economic independence. Whether you're launching a business in Lagos, investing in property in Accra, or exploring ecotourism ventures in Tanzania, the goal should be sustainable prosperity that benefits both individuals and the larger African community.

Embracing a Pan-African Lifestyle

A Pan-African lifestyle is about more than geography; it is about unity, cultural exchange, and the commitment to an Africa without borders in heart and mind. The

African Union recognizes six regions: North, South, East, West, Central Africa, and the diaspora. Living The African Dream means integrating with local cultures while staying connected to the broader Pan-African community. Whether you are immersing in the vibrant rhythms of South African Amapiano, participating in cultural festivals in Kenya, or engaging in entrepreneurial projects in Botswana, the key is intentional engagement. Afrocentric Regenerative Travel champions the idea that those from the diaspora and those on the continent can exchange knowledge, skills, and wisdom for mutual growth. It is about learning from African traditions while also bringing fresh perspectives, innovations, and expertise from the diaspora to enhance and expand opportunities.

Wellness & Community

Thriving in Africa also means prioritizing well-being—physically, mentally, and emotionally. Wellness is deeply embedded in African cultures, from indigenous herbal medicine and holistic healing in Namibia to mindfulness practices inspired by spiritual traditions across the continent. Access to quality healthcare, fitness, and wellness resources is vital to maintaining a balanced lifestyle. Community is at the heart of African living, and building relationships is essential for long-term success. Whether through local networks, expat groups, business associations, or grassroots initiatives, the ability to integrate and form meaningful connections will enrich your experience. The African Dream is sustained through collaboration, whether by mentoring young entrepreneurs in Ghana, supporting education initiatives in Tanzania, or contributing to sustainability projects in Kenya.

Final Thoughts

Africa is not just a place to relocate—it is a place to grow, to give, and to build a meaningful legacy. The journey does not end with settling into a new home; it continues through active participation in the continent's evolution. By embracing Afrocentric Regenerative Travel, practicing conscious capitalism, and fully immersing in a Pan-African lifestyle, you contribute to a future where Africa thrives as a beacon of innovation, unity, and prosperity. This guide has provided the foundation, but the real adventure is yours to create. Welcome home to Africa, where your dreams, purpose, and legacy can take root and flourish.

FINAL THOUGHT

The African proverb **"A strong tree shall always grow from the roots and not the seeds"** beautifully encapsulates the journey outlined in *Africa 101: The Pan-African Lifestyle Guide to Relocating, Investing & Living The African Dream in the Motherland.* This book serves as the foundation—the roots—providing you with the essential knowledge, insights, and tools to plant your seed in Africa.

But planting the seed is only the beginning. To truly live *The African Dream* and embrace a Pan-African lifestyle, you must do the work to establish deep roots. These roots symbolize commitment, resilience, and a deep connection to the culture, history, and opportunities of the Motherland. Only with strong roots can the tree grow tall and bear the fruit of your dreams—a life of purpose, prosperity, and unity within the vibrant tapestry of Africa.

Now, it's your turn. Let the guidance in this book inspire you to plant your seed, nurture your roots, and grow something extraordinary. Together, we can cultivate a future where *The African Dream* flourishes, and the true essence of the Pan-African lifestyle thrives.

.

LIVE THE AFRICAN DREAM

Africa 101

GENERAL CONTINENT BRIEF

Africa is a vast and dynamic continent undergoing rapid transformation across all sectors—social, political, economic, and cultural. With 54 recognized countries, a fast-growing population, and a wealth of natural and human resources, Africa is poised to play a leading role in shaping the future of the world.

The continent is home to a deeply spiritual and culturally rich population. The top religions in Africa include **Christianity**, **Islam**, and **African Traditional Spirituality**, all of which play a significant role in shaping values, customs, and daily life. Social and political life on the continent tends to be **conservative**, with strong reverence for **tradition, elders, and ancestral heritage**. Many African societies uphold **traditional family values**, with an emphasis on the **family nucleus**, respect for lineage, and community responsibility.

In terms of governance and business, **personal relationships**, **networking**, and in many cases **lobbying or high persuasion**, are often necessary to navigate political and economic systems effectively. While these systems are evolving, they reflect a long-standing cultural focus on negotiation, diplomacy, and relational influence.

Simultaneously, Africa is experiencing a **powerful Pan-African renaissance**. Across the continent and within the diaspora, there is growing momentum toward greater **unity, integration, and shared vision**. While individuals and communities maintain diverse personal beliefs and religious practices, a shared desire for a **united, self-determined, and prosperous Africa** is becoming a leading priority. This movement is not just ideological—it is being translated into economic partnerships, cultural exchange, and systemic efforts to strengthen Africa politically, socially, and economically for the benefit of all people of African descent globally.

Disclaimer:
This information is rapidly evolving. While all efforts have been made to ensure the data presented is accurate, the statistics and rankings are based on the best available sources as of 2025. Factors such as population, economy, safety, and infrastructure are subject to change over time.

Overview

Africa is the **second-largest** and **second-most-populous** continent on Earth. Covering about **30.3 million km² (11.7 million square miles)** — including its adjacent islands — it makes up **20% of Earth's land area** and around **6% of its total surface area.**

As of **2021**, Africa had a population of nearly **1.4 billion people**, accounting for approximately **18% of the world's human population.** By **2050**, Africa is projected to have the **largest** and **youngest** population on the planet, with a **median age below 30**.

Africa's potential is immense. It's the **most mineral-rich continent** on Earth, boasting vast reserves of gold, diamonds, cobalt, oil, lithium, and other rare earth minerals. Equally valuable is its **human capital**, making Africa the future powerhouse of the global economy.

The African Union recognizes the **African Diaspora as the "sixth region"** of the continent, acknowledging the historical and ongoing contributions of people of African descent worldwide. There's a **growing and powerful economic and political bond between Africa and the Caribbean**, rooted in shared ancestry, solidarity, and aspirations for Pan-African unity and empowerment.

Africa as a Collectivist Society

Africa, in its broad diversity, is known for its **collectivist** nature, where community, shared responsibility, and interconnectedness are at the heart of many cultures. Unlike **individualistic societies**, where personal achievement is often the central focus, African cultures typically emphasize the importance of **the collective good—** the well-being of the group, whether family, village, or broader society. African societies have long placed a high value on **social relationships**, often greeting strangers in passing and considering it strange not to acknowledge others.

Elders hold a place of profound respect across the continent. In many cultures, elders are addressed with titles such as **"ma"**, **"mama"**, **"sir"**, or **"dad"**, signaling their wisdom and role within the family structure. This respect extends beyond biological ties, as titles like **"uncle"** and **"auntie"** are used for well-known community members, regardless of familial connection. Parents, too, are deeply respected, and there is a general recognition of the **familial bond** that binds people together.

Non-Indigenous Populations in Africa: A Complex Relationship

Africa, the ancestral homeland of Black people, has long been shaped by the resilience, brilliance, and unity of its indigenous communities. However, the continent is also home to **non-indigenous populations**—those who are **not of African descent**, including people of **European, Asian, and Middle Eastern** heritage. These groups began settling in various parts of Africa primarily through **colonial occupation**, **trade networks**, and **migration**.

Demographic Overview

As of mid-2020, Africa hosted an estimated **40.6 million international migrants**, representing approximately **14.5% of the global migrant population**. Of these, around **21 million Africans** were living in another African country, indicating significant intra-continental migration.

In **South Africa**, a prominent destination for migrants, there were about **2.4 million foreign-born residents** in 2022, with significant numbers from neighboring African countries.

While specific numbers of non-African foreigners (i.e., individuals not of African descent) are less readily available, it is evident that African countries host diverse populations from around the world.

Historical and Ongoing Tensions

The presence of non-indigenous communities is often linked to **colonial systems of land ownership, political power, and economic control**, structures that persist today. This has resulted in **historically tense and often unequal relationships** between these foreign ethnic groups and indigenous African populations.

In several countries, non-indigenous communities maintain **disproportionate control over industries, prime real estate, and major businesses**, with minimal integration into or respect for the surrounding African communities.

While there are **exceptions**—individuals within these groups who actively support African development and engage in respectful cross-cultural relationships—the general trend has been **one-sided**. Many of these communities have built **insular networks**, operating parallel to the majority society and often **excluding** African people from opportunities in land ownership, business partnerships, and shared community leadership. These exclusionary practices are especially visible in certain suburbs, industries, and economic corridors, where **Africans are underrepresented or outright marginalized**.

Moreover, the approach to community development by some of these groups can be described as **expansionist**, often focused on economic growth and land acquisition for their benefit rather than fostering genuine partnerships with the local populations.

Countries with the Highest Numbers of Foreign-Born Residents

The countries below have the largest populations of non-indigenous foreigners. These figures are based on available data at the time of this publication and are subject to rapid change due to migration patterns, regional development, and shifting economic dynamics:

- **South Africa** – Approx. 2.86 million foreign-born residents. Includes 800,000 of Indian descent, around 350,000 Chinese, and sizable European-origin populations.

- **Côte d'Ivoire** – Approx. 2.56 million foreigners. Home to an estimated 80,000–300,000 Lebanese residents.

- **Nigeria** – Approx. 1.31 million foreigners, including Chinese, Lebanese, and Indian populations.

- **Kenya** – Approx. 1.05 million foreigners. Significant Indian and Chinese communities.

- **Angola** – Approx. 259,000 Chinese residents, primarily concentrated in Luanda.

- **Zambia and Madagascar** – Each host over 100,000 Chinese nationals.

- **Senegal** – Lebanese population estimated between 15,000 and 30,000.

- **Mozambique** – Hosts an estimated 70,000 people of Indian descent.

- **Uganda** – Approx. 1.72 million foreigners.

- **Ethiopia** – Approx. 1.09 million foreigners.

- **Sudan** – Approx. 1.38 million foreigners.

- **Democratic Republic of Congo** – Approx. 950,000 foreigners.

- **South Sudan** – Approx. 880,000 foreigners.

- **Libya** – Approx. 830,000 foreigners.

These examples are not exhaustive and reflect trends at a specific moment in time. Migration and regional investment continue to reshape these figures across the continent.

Race Relations, Colorism, Texturism, and Tribalism

While Africa's diverse peoples are often united in shared cultural pride and Pan-African solidarity, there are still **internal tensions** that hinder complete unity. These tensions stem from historical systems of **racial division, colorism, texturism**, and **tribalism**, remnants of colonialism and the ongoing struggle for sovereignty and identity.

- Colorism: In some African communities, lighter skin tones are still favored over darker skin, a vestige of colonial influence and the legacy of the **"divide and conquer"** tactics used by colonial powers to create divisions among Africans.

- Texturism: Similarly, there has been a history of preference for straighter hair textures over tightly coiled or natural hair, a result of the deep-rooted influence of Eurocentric beauty standards.

Tribalism also remains an issue in some parts of Africa, where historical ethnic conflicts and divisions are sometimes exploited for political gain. Yet, despite these challenges, a growing movement among **younger generations** of Africans is actively moving beyond these divisive ideologies. Many are more focused on **unity**, shared cultural identity, and **Africa's progress on the global stage**.

That said, some African communities still experience areas where **exclusionary practices** persist, with certain neighborhoods or industries **dominated by foreign-owned businesses**, often alienating local African communities. This tension is linked to broader issues of **neocolonialism**—the continued influence of foreign powers in economic and political affairs, making it difficult for indigenous Africans to thrive.

Pan-Africanism and Tensions Between North Africa and Sub-Saharan Africa

Another point of tension within the African continent lies in the ongoing debates surrounding **North Africa and Sub-Saharan Africa**. In some parts of **North Africa**, there exists a belief among certain populations that they are more **Arab** than African, a viewpoint that has led to **cultural and racial tensions** between North Africans and **Sub-Saharan Africans**. Some individuals identify as **both Arab and African**, embracing a broader Pan-African identity.

This division is not universal across the continent, as many Africans in **East Africa** and the **Horn of Africa** also grapple with similar identity questions, especially as **Arab influence** and **Islam** play a prominent role in shaping the region. However, the Pan-African movement continues to challenge these divisions, with younger Africans recognizing the need for solidarity across all of Africa, regardless of ethnicity, religion, or geographical location.

In places like **Mauritius**, **Comoros Island**, and **Seychelles**, mixed populations have evolved, blending African and Asian ancestries, with some individuals having both **Indian and African** backgrounds. These communities continue to build **Pan-African unity**, valuing the diverse heritage and history that connects them to the broader African story.

Relationships and Marriage in African Culture

Marriage and relationships in Africa are built on a foundation of **respect, family unity**, and **community involvement**. Many African cultures place great value on **courting**, which is a process of getting to know one another with the **involvement of families**. The act of presenting oneself to the **family** is an essential part of **African marriage customs**, emphasizing the **importance of family approval** in union formation.

A significant part of the marriage tradition is the **dowry**. Contrary to some portrayals in mainstream media, the **dowry** is not a **"bride price"**. Instead, it is a gesture of respect and appreciation toward the woman's family for raising her. The dowry symbolizes the recognition of the woman's departure from her family as she begins a new life with her spouse. It is also a celebration of the **union between two families**. The dowry varies from culture to culture, with some communities requesting symbolic gifts such as wine, while others ask for items like **cows** or **specific textiles**, depending on cultural preferences.

In African tradition, the **traditional wedding** is often considered more important than the **civil ceremony**, as it is deeply connected to cultural heritage and represents the union of both families and communities. Traditional weddings are full of vibrant **cultural attire**, music, and dance, representing the **communal nature** of African culture.

Countries of Africa

Country	Region	Independence Date
Algeria	North	July 5, 1962
Angola	Central	Nov 11, 1975
Benin	West	Aug 1, 1960
Botswana	South	Sep 30, 1966
Burkina Faso	West	Aug 5, 1960
Burundi	East	July 1, 1962

Country	Region	Independence Date
Cabo Verde	West	July 5, 1975
Cameroon	Central	Jan 1, 1960
Central African Republic	Central	Aug 13, 1960
Chad	Central	Aug 11, 1960
Comoros	East	July 6, 1975
Congo (Brazzaville)	Central	Aug 15, 1960
Congo (DRC)	Central	June 30, 1960
Côte d'Ivoire	West	Aug 7, 1960
Djibouti	East	June 27, 1977
Egypt	North	Feb 28, 1922 (Republic: 1953)
Equatorial Guinea	Central	Oct 12, 1968
Eritrea	East	May 24, 1993
Eswatini	South	Sep 6, 1968
Ethiopia	East	Never colonized (recognized 1941)
Gabon	Central	Aug 17, 1960

Country	Region	Independence Date
Gambia	West	Feb 18, 1965
Ghana	West	March 6, 1957
Guinea	West	Oct 2, 1958
Guinea-Bissau	West	Sep 24, 1973
Kenya	East	Dec 12, 1963
Lesotho	South	Oct 4, 1966
Liberia	West	July 26, 1847
Libya	North	Dec 24, 1951
Madagascar	East	June 26, 1960
Malawi	East	July 6, 1964
Mali	West	Sep 22, 1960
Mauritania	West	Nov 28, 1960
Mauritius	East	March 12, 1968
Morocco	North	March 2, 1956
Mozambique	South	June 25, 1975
Namibia	South	March 21, 1990
Niger	West	Aug 3, 1960

Country	Region	Independence Date
Nigeria	West	Oct 1, 1960
Rwanda	East	July 1, 1962
São Tomé and Príncipe	Central	July 12, 1975
Senegal	West	April 4, 1960
Seychelles	East	June 29, 1976
Sierra Leone	West	April 27, 1961
Somalia	East	July 1, 1960
South Africa	South	May 31, 1910 (Republic: 1961)
South Sudan	East	July 9, 2011
Sudan	North	Jan 1, 1956
Tanzania	East	Dec 9, 1961
Togo	West	April 27, 1960
Tunisia	North	March 20, 1956
Uganda	East	Oct 9, 1962
Zambia	South	Oct 24, 1964

Country	Region	Independence Date
Zimbabwe	South	April 18, 1980

Languages in Africa

- **Most Popular Non-Indigenous Languages (By Number of Countries Spoken):**

    1. French – spoken in 31 countries

    2. English – spoken in 27 countries

    3. Arabic – widely used in North Africa and the Sahel

- **Most Spoken Indigenous Language:**

    o Kiswahili (Swahili) – Over 100 million speakers across East, Central, and Southern Africa. Recognized by the African Union as Africa's continental language.

Top African Rankings (As of 2025)

Safest African Countries

Mauritius, Botswana, Namibia, Seychelles, Ghana, Rwanda, Morocco, Zambia, Tanzania, Senegal

Most Populated

Nigeria, Ethiopia, Egypt, DR Congo, Tanzania, South Africa, Kenya, Uganda, Sudan, Algeria

Most Visited

Morocco, Egypt, South Africa, Tunisia, Kenya, Tanzania, Zimbabwe, Ghana, Ethiopia, Mauritius

Best African Passports

Seychelles, Mauritius, South Africa, Botswana, Namibia, Lesotho, Eswatini, Kenya, Malawi, Tanzania

Most Politically Stable

Mauritius, Botswana, Ghana, Namibia, Seychelles, Cape Verde, Morocco, Senegal, Zambia, Rwanda

Cleanest

Rwanda, Mauritius, Botswana, Seychelles, Namibia, Ghana, Morocco, Tunisia, South Africa, Kenya

Largest Economies (Total GDP)

Nigeria, South Africa, Egypt, Algeria, Ethiopia, Kenya, Morocco, Ghana, Angola, Tanzania

Highest GDP per Capita

Seychelles, Mauritius, Gabon, Botswana, South Africa, Namibia, Algeria, Egypt, Morocco, Tunisia

Most Millionaires

South Africa, Egypt, Nigeria, Kenya, Morocco, Mauritius, Ghana, Tanzania, Uganda, Namibia

Most Structured / Best for Retirement

Mauritius, South Africa, Morocco, Namibia, Ghana, Botswana, Kenya, Tunisia, Rwanda, Seychelles

Best for Entrepreneurship

Nigeria, South Africa, Kenya, Egypt, Ghana, Rwanda, Morocco, Tunisia, Senegal, Uganda

---

Africa: A Continent of Endless Opportunity for Strategic Builders and Visionaries

Africa is one of the most promising business frontiers in the world today. With a youthful population, rapid urbanization, a rising middle class, and rich natural resources, the continent offers dynamic opportunities for investors and entrepreneurs of all kinds. Whether you're building from the ground up or scaling into new markets, success depends on your capital, execution, adaptability, resourcefulness, and ability to supply real solutions.

The African market doesn't reward the biggest—it rewards the boldest and most strategic. Those who take time to engage, study local dynamics, understand consumer behavior, and respond to real needs will find that Africa not only welcomes innovation—it thrives on it.

A Full Spectrum: From Small to Large-Scale Business Ventures

Africa is a place where businesses of all sizes can flourish—from micro-enterprises and family-owned shops to

multinational ventures and infrastructure megaprojects.
There's room for:

- Small and Medium Enterprises (SMEs) such as:

    o Restaurants and cafés

    o Spas and wellness centers

    o Car dealerships and auto services

    o Pharmacies and community clinics

    o Fashion boutiques and beauty salons

    o Barbershops and hair care brands

    o Food delivery and logistics platforms

    o Digital marketing, social media, and content creation agencies

    o Local tech hubs and app development teams

- Mid-Scale Ventures including:

    o Shopping malls and retail outlets

    o Real estate leasing and property management

    o Agribusiness processing and packaging hubs

    o Waste management and recycling facilities

    o Retirement homes and assisted-living facilities

- Landscaping and green infrastructure services

- Travel agencies and concierge lifestyle services

- Transportation logistics and ride-hailing solutions

- Customer service coaching, call centers, and BPO hubs

- Large-Scale Enterprises & Mega Projects in:

  - Manufacturing and industrial zones

  - Telecommunications and digital connectivity infrastructure

  - Government construction and public infrastructure (roads, bridges, airports)

  - Clean energy (hydropower, solar, wind, and renewables)

  - Mining and ethical resource extraction

  - Cultural heritage, museums, and preservation of African history

  - National transport systems and tech-integrated delivery networks

According to recent studies, SMEs make up more than 90% of businesses in Africa, contributing up to 50% of the continent's GDP and employing about 80% of the labor force (CSIS). Meanwhile, countries like Nigeria, Kenya,

Ethiopia, South Africa, and Ghana are becoming hotspots for industrial-scale investment, fueled by infrastructure development, energy demand, digital growth, and fintech innovation.

Top Emerging and High-Impact Industries Across Africa

Here are key sectors currently thriving across the continent, with growth potential and strategic entry points:

1. Real Estate Development & Leasing
   Urban migration is surging, creating demand for affordable housing, office parks, shopping complexes, and diaspora-focused gated estates. Both short-term rentals and long-term leasing offer steady returns.

2. Agribusiness & Agritech
   Africa holds over 60% of the world's uncultivated arable land. From organic farming to smart agriculture, food processing to export chains—agribusiness remains one of the most scalable and impactful sectors.

3. Manufacturing & Industrial Parks
   With the rise of the African Continental Free Trade Area (AfCFTA), local production is being incentivized. Opportunities exist in packaging, garments, building materials, electronics, and pharmaceuticals.

4. Technology & Innovation
   Tech in Africa is booming. Opportunities include:

- Ride-hailing and transportation apps (à la Bolt, SafeBoda)

- Food and grocery delivery platforms

- Healthcare apps and telemedicine

- Mobile money, payment solutions, and fintech

- E-commerce and logistics tech

- Edtech and online learning platforms

5. Telecommunications & Connectivity
   With over 1 billion mobile phone subscriptions, Africa is leapfrogging into the digital age. Investments in 4G/5G, fiber optics, rural internet expansion, and smart devices are skyrocketing.

6. Customer Service & Call Centers
   With English, French, Arabic, Swahili, and Portuguese widely spoken, Africa is poised to become a global call center destination. Investing in training and etiquette coaching is a lucrative support industry.

7. Waste Management & Environmental Services
   Sustainable collection, recycling, and even waste-to-energy solutions are being adopted in growing cities. There is strong demand for clean, reliable, and efficient waste solutions.

8. Transportation & Logistics
   From bike delivery to electric buses, Africa's

logistics networks are evolving. Apps that track fleets, digitize delivery, or serve last-mile logistics are in high demand.

9. Travel, Tourism & Concierge Services
    With Africa becoming more attractive to diaspora tourists and global travelers, there's a rising need for:

    o   Lifestyle concierge services

    o   Medical and wellness tourism

    o   Luxury travel packages

    o   Private airport transfers and curated cultural tours

10. Retirement & Assisted Living
    The aging population within the African diaspora is creating opportunities for modern retirement homes and wellness-focused care facilities, especially in peaceful, scenic regions.

11. Contracting & Major Infrastructure
    Roads, railways, ports, and government-backed construction are vital to Africa's next phase of development. Public-private partnerships are encouraged for strategic, long-term players.

12. Hydropower & Clean Energy
    From solar microgrids to large-scale wind and hydropower plants, Africa is embracing energy independence. Countries like Kenya, Rwanda, Morocco, and Ethiopia are leading the charge.

13. Mining & Ethical Resource Extraction
    The continent remains rich in gold, cobalt, lithium, bauxite, and rare earths. There is rising demand for transparent, community-conscious mining operations.

14. Cultural Heritage, Museums & Preservation
    Investment in preserving and curating African history offers cultural and tourism value. Building museums, heritage trails, and cultural education centers contributes to identity and global understanding.

Conclusion: Build With Intention, Execute with Excellence

Africa is not a monolith—it's a continent of 54 distinct nations, each with its own unique challenges and strengths. But what they all share is immense potential for those who come in with a clear mission, bold vision, and community-centered execution.

Whether you're building a small neighborhood restaurant, developing the next pan-African delivery app, or managing infrastructure contracts—Africa has a place for you. It's not just about how much you invest—it's how well you execute, how you solve a need, and how you connect with the people.

Be resourceful. Be solution-oriented. Study the market, align with local needs, and build with purpose.
Africa is not just an opportunity—it's the future.

BUSINESS PARTNERS

TM

Our Partners in Pan-African Empowerment

Diaspora Freedom Initiative
Specialists in Generational Wealth Planning, African Relocation & Business Expansion.

Diaspora Freedom Initiative, guides perfect-fit clients in building prosperous lives and ventures in Kenya, offering personalized expertise and unwavering support every step of the way. With a strong focus on long-term impact, DFI helps members of the African diaspora reconnect with their roots while establishing generational wealth through strategic relocation and enterprise development.

Traverze Culture
A dynamic lifestyle and travel consultancy dedicated to promoting Pan-African unity through curated cultural experiences, concierge services, and relocation support.

With operations across Africa, Canada, and the Caribbean, Traverze Culture empowers global Africans to explore, relocate, invest, and thrive across the continent, with a focus on sustainability, hospitality, and cultural connection.

Together, **Diaspora Freedom Initiative** and **Traverze Culture** partner with **Pan African Lifestyle (PAL)** to champion a modern, borderless African identity— encouraging global Africans to travel, invest, and live The African Dream on the continent.

FEATURED EXPERT BIO

Kea Wakesho Simmons is a pioneering businesswoman, seasoned travel and relocation expert, and certified medical tourism facilitator. As the founder and CEO of Traverze Culture, she leads a movement that connects the global Black diaspora with their ancestral roots, particularly focusing on Africa, especially Kenya. Kea's journey began with her service as a human resources specialist in the U.S. Army, where her deployments sparked a deep passion for travel. This passion, combined with her background in HR and consulting, paved the way for her to become a leading voice in the travel and relocation industry, with a particular focus on connecting Black people around the world with meaningful cultural exchanges.

Kea is proud of her Gullah Geechee roots, which play a significant role in her work today. As a trailblazer in the cultural exchange space, she has established a unique business that not only impacts Africa but also the Black diaspora globally, fostering connections between Black communities around the world and their African counterparts. Through Traverze Culture, Kea facilitates relocation, travel, and medical tourism, with a primary focus on helping African Americans reconnect with their roots in Africa. Her work is grounded in the principles of Afrocentric Regenerative Travel (ART), a philosophy that emphasizes community, collaboration, and conscious capitalism. This mindset advocates for sustainable travel and relocation practices that create lasting positive impacts for both travelers and the communities they engage with.

In addition to her role as a leader in travel, Kea is also committed to cultural preservation and exchange, bringing together the histories, roots, and unity of indigenous Black people worldwide. She advocates for mutual support and understanding, connecting diverse

Black communities through shared heritage. Kea's pioneering efforts in African travel, government consulting, medical tourism, cultural preservation, and cultural exchange continue to shape the future of global Black unity and empowerment. Through Traverze Culture, she is helping thousands of people reconnect with Africa, promoting conscious and sustainable capitalism, and making a lasting impact on Black communities around the world.

AUTHORS BIO

Emmanuel and Solange Bope are visionary leaders, entrepreneurs, and cultural ambassadors dedicated to fostering Pan-African unity and economic empowerment. As the authors of *Africa 101: The Pan-African Lifestyle Guide to Relocating, Investing & Living The African Dream in the Motherland, Live The African Dream*, and *Afrifluence*, they provide invaluable insights for those seeking to reconnect with Africa and thrive within its rich cultural and economic landscape.

The Bopes are also the founders of PANAFRICON, the world's first major Pan-African Conference, and the PAL App, the premier Pan-African Lifestyle social media platform. Through these groundbreaking initiatives, they empower the global diaspora to relocate, travel, invest, and engage in meaningful cultural exchange. Their work is built upon the pillars of Culture, Connection, Community, and Collective Capital— ensuring that the Pan-African vision is not only preserved but also advanced into the digital era. Leading Pan African Lifestyle (PAL), the foremost Pan-African media company and lifestyle brand, they have established themselves as the preeminent figures in social media, branding, and marketing within the Pan-African and global Black space.

Hailing from the Democratic Republic of the Congo, Emmanuel and Solange spent their formative years in Canada, where they met, married, and embarked on their journey as partners in life and business. With a steadfast commitment to God and family, they transplanted their aspirations to the African soil, establishing the headquarters of Pan African Lifestyle in the motherland. They have cultivated a vibrant community of PALs (Pan African Lifestylers) and have disseminated their expertise in social media, marketing, and branding to Afrifluencers worldwide, inspiring a movement of African entrepreneurship and digital influence.

Emmanuel Bope, an astute business luminary and creative visionary, spearheads PAL as its CEO and co-founder. Armed with a diploma in Public Relations, a diploma in Marketing Communication, and a degree in Marketing Science, he orchestrates PAL's strategic direction with unparalleled acumen. His expertise in digital transformation, media, and global cultural exchange has played a crucial role in shaping innovative solutions for Pan-African connectivity and economic growth.

Solange Bope, a dynamic force of creativity, thrives on innovation and impact, forging emotional connections through brand and narrative. She is the President and co-founder of Pan African Lifestyle Inc. With a background as an entrepreneur and fashionista, she infuses PAL's ventures with her flair for style and storytelling. Holding diplomas in Fashion Styling and Image Consulting, as well as Marketing Communications, she brings a unique blend of artistry and business acumen to the PAL ecosystem. Her leadership in social impact initiatives and sustainable development ensures that their projects drive positive change across the continent.

Together, Emmanuel and Solange Bope stand as exemplars of Pan-Africanism, prioritizing the development of the motherland while cherishing their roles as life partners, confidants, and parents. Their unwavering dedication to forging a new narrative for Africa through media underscores their commitment to shaping a brighter future for the continent and its people. Today, the Bopes serve as brand and media consultants, keynote speakers, entrepreneurs, and philanthropists focused on inspiring *The African Dream* and leading Pan-Africanism into the digital era.